QUIET MIND **EPIC LIFE**

QUIET MIND EPIC LIFE

ESCAPE THE STATUS QUO AND
EXPERIENCE ENLIGHTENED
PROSPERITY NOW

MATTHEW FERRY

Spiritual Hooligan Publishing Company
A division of Elevate The Vibe, LLC
2618 San Miguel Drive #100
Newport Beach, CA 92660

Second Edition
Copyright © 2019 Matthew Ferry & Elevate The Vibe LLC
All Rights Reserved

Printed in the United States of America

Accolades

"This book is filled with practical value as opposed to the typical "feel good" material that passes through the inspirational/spiritual circuit. If I could give more than 5 stars, you can trust that I would. Highly recommend!"

- Ciji Siddons

"Give yourself the GREATEST GIFT by reading this book, employing his strategies and recommending it to all of your like minded friends, for we are all connected as one."

- Jay Campbell

"So many other books I've read have so much rhetoric and fluff. But not this book. Matthew outlines the exact strategies and path to living an Enlightened life. After following his strategies in the book, I've been able to tame my ego and take major strides forward in my life."

- David Keesee

"The principles in Matthew Ferry's book have truly changed my life. I recommend Quiet Mind Epic Life to anyone desiring real information with no hype."

- Carol Butler

"It is not often you come across such a heart felt read."

- Jeff Adler

Dedication
I would like to dedicate this book to

...my teachers who were so instrumental on my path to enlightenment.

To Steven Sadleir, my friend, my teacher, and my guide. Your devotion to me was one of the most enriching aspects of my 20's and 30's. It was with you that I first entered into the state of oneness permanently. I am forever grateful.

To Dr. David Hawkins, you were my teacher from afar. I wish that I could have called you a friend. Your work has so deeply influenced my life and my process. To measure consciousness was one of the most influential aspects of my own ascent. I only got to see you speak four times before you died and being in your presence was truly uplifting. I wish you were here, so you could read these words and see the latest expression of enlightenment that your work has given birth to.

To Lane Lowry, my brother from another mother. Wow. The investigations we had together. The mind boggling assent into higher states that occurred from the collaboration we had was by far the most enlightening, interesting and epic thing I have ever experienced. My methodology would be less than what it is today without your creativity, your intuition, your mentorship, your guidance, your collaboration and your extreme commitment to curiosity.

To my wife, Kristen. If it weren't for you, I would still be teaching people sales and wishing I was teaching what I really knew and understood. You helped me restore my integrity and well being. You were instrumental in helping me see my blind spots and how my own 'misperceptions' were stopping me from being the leader I felt so compelled to be. Baby... Let's do this!

Dedication: I would like to dedicate this book to

Table of Contents

PART FOUR: DAILY PRACTICES

PART FIVE: APPENDIX & GLOSSARY

Introduction
Welcome To Quiet Mind Epic Life

"When your mind is free from the distractions created by resistance, you are free to create your dream life."

A quiet mind is a peaceful mind not burdened by negative chatter and unwanted interruptions. A quiet mind is the platform for creating an epic life.

If I do my job right and you read every word of this book, then your mind will go quiet for long periods of time. Not forever. *This isn't a quick fix cure to an over-active mind.*

Instead, I am about to give you a series of perspectives and practices that will steadily reduce your mind chatter until you achieve what I call Quiet Mind Epic Life.

When your mind is quiet, you see things clearly. You stop resisting other people and the circumstances of life. You stop believing and adhering to the illogical standards that make sure you feel less than. With a quiet mind, you are finally free from the irrational fears that cause self-sabotage.

Here's my promise. The more you implement what I am about to teach you, the more fearless you will become. And that is a good thing! Fearlessness creates a big boost in your confidence. It has the power to improve almost every area of your life. The deeper you get into this process, the faster you are going to get that pep back in your step. As a result, you'll find yourself smiling more and enjoying life.

When you feel free and relaxed, your curiosity becomes insatiable. Suddenly, you feel compelled to go after the meaningful goals that create your version of an epic life.

Throughout this book, we are going to focus on your perspective. The ability to control your perspective is the foundation to becoming an enlightened being. That's my ultimate goal for you.

Practicing the perspectives in this book will help you to transcend the insanity of your mind. When that happens, you have achieved what is traditionally called Enlightenment.

Together we are going to use a methodology that has taken me 20+ years to develop called The Rapid Enlightenment Process.

Enlightenment is not a religion. Enlightenment is a mindset of sorts. It's a very practical way of looking at the world that makes fearlessness possible. It makes many other things possible too. Let me give you my definition of Enlightenment... so you understand our endgame together.

> *"Enlightenment is the recognition that the source of life within you is also the source of life in everyone and everything else. We are all one thing expressing itself with infinite variety."*

When you truly see that the source of life within you is also the source of life in everyone and everything else. When you see that we are all one thing expressing itself with infinite variety... and the only thing that makes us different... is our perspective about it... then, BOOM!

In that moment, everything changes. Fear disappears. Suddenly you realize there is no reason to be afraid. You instantly recognize that if the source of life in you is the source of everything, then there is nothing to fear, resist, avoid, repel, change or otherwise fight against.

In this state, you suddenly forgive everyone for everything. You stop resisting and you start appreciating.

You appreciate the good things. The bad things. The breakthroughs and the breakdowns. They all suddenly seem perfect in the grand scheme.

> *Recognizing the perfection of everything creates an immediate feeling of peace. You find yourself smiling all the time.*

In your enlightened state, stress, worry, and fear become irrelevant. They don't make sense to you anymore.

Enlightenment is very practical. When worry and fear become irrelevant "You are free to move about the cabin people!" You are free to create the life you want. You are unbound. You are free.

From this new perspective that the source of life within you, is the source of life in everyone and everything, you rise above the limitations of cultural conditioning. You don't have to follow the rules anymore. Everything is up for evaluation. You see the dogma for what it is: Stories, made up by well-meaning people. But stories nonetheless. Not valid. Not true. Not real. You feel free. The invisible barriers disappear.

When your mind is quiet, your limiting beliefs feel like a bad joke that you were playing on yourself. You laugh at the beliefs you used to have, and naturally, effortlessly, they stop limiting you.

A quiet mind state is an enlightened state. When you are enlightened you recognize that you are infinite and you know it. With nothing distracting you in your mind, you feel your unlimited nature. You recognize that you are in a body and it has limitations but your intuition tells you that you are not your body and you are unlimited.

With a quiet mind, all that stuff that you used to resist about yourself, the stuff you used to resist about the people in your life, about your job, about your family... poof... that resistance no longer makes sense.

If you are them, and they are you, if we are all one thing expressing itself with infinite variety, then resistance seems silly. As a result, it just melts away in your Enlightened Perspective.

Now... Don't get me wrong.

The world is still the same world from before. There are still disasters, breakdowns, failure, and misunderstandings. People still get upset with you, and your projects still fail. There are still politics, crime, bad behavior and natural disasters, but in an enlightened state, hardly anything bugs you or takes you off your game.

When your mind is free from the clutter created by resistance, agitation, annoyances, doubts, fears, uncertainty... you are free to focus on what matters. You aren't distracted by the mind's obsession with looking good, being right, judging people, avoiding negativity, or being popular.

All that suffering caused by your judgments subsides.

You are no longer burdened by lamenting thoughts like "Am I doing it right? Do they like me? Am I going to succeed? Am I good enough?"

In your enlightened state, all that mental chatter is transcended and you are freakishly free - wildly free - more free than you have ever been in your life.

Why? Think about it like this: When you are enlightened you see things as they are. You see that we are all one thing expressing itself with an infinite variety.

You are no longer subject to the influence of your perceptual filters and stories your mind tells you. This creates the ability to maintain a calm and peaceful state in a chaotic and uncertain world. Can you imagine a world where almost nothing takes you off your game?

That is very practical. Thank you for joining me on this journey.

Matthew Ferry

Chapter 1
Looking for Enlightenment in All the Wrong Places

In a moment I am going to make a crazy claim. What I'm about to say has been proven to be true for me and the people that I've helped over the last few decades. Are you ready?

Here we go.

The ability to master the process that I will teach you in this book will free you from ever having to read another self-help book. Ever. *Unless you are inspired to do so.*

That's crazy talk, right? Wrong!

My friend, you are at the end of the line. This is the pinnacle. All other self-help seminars, books, and audios are about to become irrelevant to your life.

I know. I know. It's an audacious claim. But you are going to discover that I am a fanatic about integrity and making sure to deliver on every single claim I make. The claim above is one that I stand behind with intense vigor. Why? Because self-help is *not* a guaranteed way to attain peace of mind, joy, fearlessness, calm, prosperity or satisfaction.

Yet, if you investigate why you love self-help, you will find that you are hoping it will lead to peace of mind, joy, fearlessness, calm, prosperity and satisfaction. Sorry, self-help won't get you all the way up that mountain.

Let's do a gut check together.

Book after book and seminar after seminar, promise the quantum leap - the seemingly attainable, but just out of your reach, phenomenon where diligent students like you and me will wake up and KABAM! Our professional life is rocking, our bank account is fat, we are thin, healthy, in great relationships, and feeling unstoppable.

It's like suddenly, we've graduated. Some magic switch got flipped, and all the hard work, time, energy, money, optimism, and positive thinking have paid off. It's as if we've been catapulted into the ranks of the super successful.

We imagine being on stage with our favorite teacher, the shining example of a student who made it, whose perpetual success is guaranteed by having broken through the challenging times. The student who finally has the peace of mind because they've "made it."

But you and I know that's not really how it is.

In this chapter, I want to explore why self-help, which has made such a huge impact on who you are today, isn't helping you anymore. It was an important step in your journey, but its life-cycle is complete.

I want to open your eyes to what you have actually been seeking. My objective in this chapter is to help you have a realization about the true nature of your search. I want you to see that you have actually been looking to achieve the pinnacle of human states of consciousness called Enlightenment.

> I define Enlightenment as the recognition that the source of life within you is the source of life in everyone and everything else. We are all one thing expressing itself with infinite variety.

Enlightenment is the state of consciousness where Quiet Mind Epic Life exists.

Now, before I get ahead of myself, let's step back and examine the problems you face and why self-help isn't helping you anymore.

Over the years, I've realized that we all buy into similar self-help myths. These myths include ideas that feel completely real, but when they get put to the test, don't deliver the results they promise.

Self-Help Myth #1

"I can rewire my brain by eliminating negative thoughts and replacing them with positive thoughts."

Simply stated, self-help relies on the underlying assumption that the mind that created the problem can fix the problem.

And that's, in itself, a real problem!

How many times have you been in a good mood and something negative, out of your control, happens and... BAM! You go into a state of doubt, uncertainty, frustration or maybe even anger?

The idea of eliminating negative thoughts and replacing them with positive ones has merit, but it doesn't lead to a Quiet Mind Epic Life. It leads to a profound waste of your time. Suddenly you become the negative thought police. Your mind becomes the bad guy and you become the hero who is going to squash the mind and then rehabilitate it.

Look, I am confident that you are *much* more positive today than when you first embarked upon your self-help journey. Nevertheless, I suspect you aren't always positive if, for example, you are running late and someone aggressively takes your parking spot. Your mind would also probably get fired up if someone pretends like they didn't just cut in front of you in a line at Starbucks or the mind could replay an awkward phone call you had over and over without your permission.

These daily occurrences can be unsettling and when they happen... Poof! Your hard-earned positive thinking evaporates into thin air.

It's like your positivity bank account is suddenly wiped out, and you have no control over the deposits of negativity flooding in.

Here's a disturbing fact for you: self-help is not designed to eliminate negativity. It is designed to cover it up with positivity and optimism. That's like planting a rose garden over your sewer to try to hide the smell.

I have developed a completely different approach. **In fact, with every turn of the page in this book, you will systematically eliminate the source of negativity in your life.** As a result of this elimination, you will experience more joy and optimism.

In defense of positivity, I will say this: Applying a positive response to things that happen in life is very powerful. I'm sure that positivity lifted you out of the masses of people who are living their entire life in a sea of negativity. For that, I'm grateful to the positivity movement. But I've discovered it only takes you so far.

What you seek is far beyond rising above negativity. You seek the impact of a pervasive, quiet mind. You hope to cultivate joy, happiness, peace, creativity, and resourcefulness no matter how crazy life gets.

You will never achieve that by rewiring your mind. Your mind will always find its way back to its basic purpose. Here's the real solution.

You must remove your mind's motive for thinking.

But I am getting ahead of myself. First, let's tackle...

Self-Help Myth #2

"When I achieve my goals, I enjoy my success and I will finally have the peace I seek."

Sorry. Doesn't happen.

Success does not create happiness and is often more disruptive than enjoyable. More success can lead to more bills, more concerns, and a lot more responsibility. It can also lead to more people making requests of you, more opportunities to lose, more risk, and more complexity. All of these additions naturally lead to more complexity and stress.

Let me take you back to the beginning of my story so you can understand where I'm coming from.

I started my spiritual journey when I was 9 years old and I had several out of body experiences that changed my life forever. I was filled with a joy, a wholeness, and completeness that was so overwhelming that, once it stopped, I was filled with unbearable longing and sadness.

I became ravenous in my search to achieve that state again. In my preteens and teens, I explored religion. I read books. I explored new age techniques. I started using psychedelic drugs and sex trying to get back there again. Nothing seemed to work.

Then it happened. After a failed recording contract in my late teens (long story, but yes, I dreamed of being a rock star as a kid), I started working for my first true mentor, my father, Mike Ferry.

In the 1970s, my dad founded the nation's top real estate sales training company. He was inspired to mentor others by his own mentor, Earl Nightingale, one of the grandfathers of the self-help movement in the 60's. My father, and now me, come from a long line of personal development authors, trainers, and philosophers.

Under my father's wing, I was sent to every training, every workshop and every seminar he could find. He hired the best coaches and consultants to guide my development. As a result, I was hooked. I started studying self-help night and day.

Through this exposure, I became convinced that success was the answer. If I achieved my goals, I would organically become happy! Maybe this would get me back to that joyous state I experienced when I was 9 years old?

At the time it made sense. I saw shining examples of successful people who seemed to be very happy. They seemed to have it all. The good life, the relationships, the money, the opportunities... all the things I longed for. I was convinced like I suspect you still are, that "success" is the key to happiness.

As I step back with my understanding today, I see that the books, the cassette tapes (yes, I'm old school), and the seminars all played into my fears, my desires, and that longing in my soul from 9 years old to find profound peace.

My mentors told me with extreme certainty, "When you are successful, you will be happy. You will have it all, you will be fulfilled, and you will have made it." They painted images of travel, cars, houses, and a life of leisure.

I'm like you - I was all in. "Game on! If success is the ticket to happiness, then that's what I'm going to achieve!"

I will tell you the whole story in the coming pages, but for now, I want to debunk this myth that success is going to create peace of mind, fulfillment, and joy.

By my late 20's and into my 30's, by all measures, I was extremely successful. I had the money, the house in a gated community, the fast cars, a motorcycle, boat, the gorgeous wife. I ran two marathons, traveled 20 weeks a year training tens of thousands of people nationwide. The money was flowing. My life *looked* really good. Unfortunately, none of that success solved the real problems that I faced. I was just as insecure as before the success.

All of those insecurities evolved into feelings of being a fraud. I would get fearful about my future. I was often disgruntled and easily triggered into negativity. I was supposed to be a super positive guy, but negativity kept overthrowing me.

For me, the promise of success didn't pan out. It didn't deliver what it promised. And this realization, I've found, to actually be quite common.

The truth is, I've helped tens of thousands of people get on the road to success. And I've helped tens of thousands of people achieve extraordinary success using tried and true self-help techniques. But none of them achieved pervasive and profound happiness and peace. They had the money. They had the life-style. They looked shiny, happy, and successful on the outside, but they were still frustrated and unsatisfied on the inside. They were constantly wondering, "When am I finally going to make it?"

The clients I trained over the last few decades (and my own life) prove that success, in all its forms, does NOT equal happiness, peace, and fulfillment. And it certainly does not produce a quiet mind.

The Unspoken Reality of the Self-Help Business

This might sound strange to you, but in my 30's, decades into my journey, I realized that self-help was a business.

With reflection, I was relating to it like it was "the truth" about life, a doctrine of sorts. I was a devotee. I did what my mentors told me to with blind faith.

I started to realize that the business function of the self-help industry was to play on my fears and my desires to motivate me to buy books, audios, seminars, and coaching material. Basically, the business wanted me to spend money. You and I are simply the target audience for a very profitable industry.

Surrounded by people in the business of self-help every day, I began to have the gut-wrenching realization that authors, speakers, teachers, and their copywriters were being paid huge sums of money to get me to buy into dreams that were, in fact, unproven and sometimes flat-out lies.

From day one, I have had a strange sense of obligation to my students. My philosophy is that I would never teach anyone something I hadn't done, and proven to work, myself. It was horrifying to find out that other people didn't have that same standard.

I don't say this to discredit or create divisiveness. In fact, I honor the role of self-help in my life and in yours. I believe it is a very very important **first step** in the journey. But, that's just it. It's a step. It is not the destination you seek.

Look, I work in the self-help industry. Here's what you can count on me for: proven steps to help you achieve Quiet Mind Epic Life.

If we are being totally honest, you and I have both benefited greatly from self-help resources. You and I have way better lives because of the books we have read, the teachers we have followed, and the techniques we have put into practice.

And yet, I am crystal clear that you don't have pervasive, profound, overwhelming peace and joy because of the successes that you have been able to achieve.

I know this because I succeeded, and it didn't fulfill on the promise. I know this because I was a teacher of success principles, and my students were still fearful, uncertain about their lives, wondering when they were going to finally achieve the, "I've made it" feeling.

Whoops! You Got Stuck in the Personal Development Prison

Have you noticed that you are on a never-ending treadmill of more books, more seminars, and more events? You keep making incremental gains, but you never really achieve that feeling of profound peace.

I hate to be the one who has to break this news to you, but you have been stuck in The Personal Development Prison.

You are confined by unexamined claims and promises about personal development that just aren't true.

Without even realizing it, you have become limited by a set of beliefs and ways of looking at the world that is fixed. You've been convinced that your personal development will lead you to the promise land...So where is it?

Wake up!!!

Enter me: slapping you in the face right now.

You're in an addictive cycle.

You are on a morphine drip.

You are the donkey with the carrot dangling just out of its reach.

The skills you've developed on your self-help journey have gotten you here, but you keep seeking, buying more books, more seminars, and more events.

You keep getting the hits of dope, but the thing is, they don't last. You probably even experience fleeting moments of happiness, joy, and peace. Fleeting moments of feeling like you've made it.

Look, I know you've got a good life, but if you are being honest, it's not really the ultimate life you know you are capable of living.

And if you are like I was, all those years ago, you can't put your finger on exactly why.

You Can't Get There From Here

Let me cut to the chase.

We all know the old adage, "Change your thinking, change your life."

Makes sense, right?

But how on earth do you do that?

How do you actually change your thinking to permanently change your life?

After years of trying and really working to gain 100% control over my mind by shoving as much personal development mate-

rial into my brain as humanly possible, I came to a stark realiza
tion.

I can try to change my thinking all I want, and my mind still dominates me with its opinions without my permission.

"You're fat." "That won't work." "Last time, you failed." "Give me a break..." "What are you doing?" "You should have..."

No matter what I did, I was unable to escape my brain's non-stop commentary.

Satisfaction? Nope! There was always something new to achieve that would finally "make me satisfied."

Peace of Mind? Nope! I was consistently robbed of my peace with my mind's need to share its opinions, concerns, judgments, and doomsday predictions.

Fearlessness? Nope! Doubt and second-guessing myself lingered no matter what I did.

Here's the bottom line: If you aren't feeling peaceful, fearless, calm, and prosperous...if you don't have the financial success, health, relationships and peace of mind that you REALLY want... then self-help isn't working for you either.

Before You Go Any Farther... You Need To Know Two Things

If you want Quiet Mind Epic Life, then you must realize...

1. Self-help lives in the realm of the mind.

2. Changing the mind is NOT the solution to attaining a quiet mind.

Let me tell you what I mean.

The path of self-help works like this:

Expose > Understand > Change

Phase 1: Expose

The moment you read your first self-help book, you are never the same. It's like someone took out a flashlight and illuminated the corner of a room you'd never see before. It's awesome, right? You and I crave that experience.

Phase 2: Understand

Now that you have a taste of what improving yourself can do, you want more. You begin to understand how the mind works and why you do what you do so you can break through to the next level.

In Phase 2 it feels *so good* to be on a journey of personal power and advancement. And if you are like me, you can't get enough. Keep it coming!

Phase 3: Change

By now, you are becoming an advanced student. You find your-self able to change your thinking in ways you never realized be-fore. Your sense of self is strong, and you are successful. People are naturally attracted to your energy and your vitality.

During Phase 3, you are eager for greater levels of control over your thoughts and reactions to life. You crave positivity and peace of mind. You want more of everything you got in Phase 2. So, you up your game and start attending live events, seminars, or weekend workshops. You are becoming a self-help veteran.

You are rocking Phase 3, baby.

Yeah! Your life is working.

Personal power and success are yours.

People love being around you.

In many ways, you are like a mystic. You put your focus on an outcome you want to achieve, and it happens. The people around you are in awe!

Then, slowly, you start to realize you aren't really advancing much anymore.

The a-ha moments are fewer and far between.

You start to notice that you've been setting the same goals for a couple of years now. Your journals are filled with different versions of the same themes around relationships, weight loss, wanting to travel, buying a new house, finally following your passion for art or non-profits, or starting a new business (in my case).

You start to wonder, "Is it me? Is my life going to stay about the same as it is now? And, if not, what's the catalyst for change?"

It's the first time you start to think, "Hmmm...Is the path I am on guaranteed to take me where I really want to go?"

Welcome to the club.

The Personal Development Prison... The Never-Ending Cycle of Phase 3

If you are reading these pages, then I know approximately where you are.

How many of these statements describe your experience?

- **Positive but not peaceful** - You still get frustrated, annoyed, and agitated by some people and situations in your life.

- **Optimistic but not overjoyed** - You know that there is a future where you feel overjoyed by all that your life is, but you admit you aren't there now.

- **Focused but not fearless** - Doubt still creeps in. Sometimes you can't get the mind to stop bugging you with its doomsday predictions.

- **Confident but not calm** - You still have little moments of worry or anxiety about your future.
- **Passionate but not prosperous** - You're a go-getter, but you wonder when money will no longer be an issue.
- **Successful but not satisfied** - You have achieved a lot. However, you can't seem to shake the feeling that you are underperforming and others are ahead of you.

You are getting this, aren't you?

I'm speaking your language, right?

This book is for you my friend. I've got your back. I've built my entire life around helping people, like you, get out of this insanity. The end of this craziness is near.

These are the *exact* insights that propelled me into a decades-long investigation into what it would take to realize the mental, emotional, spiritual, relational, and financial states I so desperately wanted in my life.

I wanted to be satisfied and eager for more, have profound peace of mind, and be fearless beyond measure!

I began to realize that self-help was a stepping stone, not the endgame.

I could count on my self-help techniques to make sure I was:

- Positive
- Optimistic

- Focused
- Passionate
- Confident
- Successful

But that still wasn't enough.

I wanted to...

- Experience profound peace
- Feel overjoyed for no reason
- Take on new projects in a fearless way
- Be prosperous in all areas of my life
- Be calm no matter what
- Experience a deep level of satisfaction day in and day out

Once I realized self-help wasn't going to get me there, I was a man on a mission to crack the code.

The same voracity behind my epic rise with personal development was now solely directed towards the only objective that mattered: a spiritual quest to achieve a quiet mind.

Chapter 2
The Spiritual Elephant in the Room

For years I searched high and low for a way to get my mind to stop distracting me with its fears, concerns, estimates and judgments. I didn't realize that I was seeking an enlightened state.

As I said in the introduction, I tried every kind of personal development process I could find. None of it created lasting peace. None of it quieted my mind.

While I became more successful in the material aspects of life, I still suffered from insecurity, doubts, and fears.

As I'll explain later, I knew that peace was possible. Very early on in my life, I had some deep mystical experiences that caused me to feel profound peace. I wanted that back!

I wanted to have an epic life and for me, that meant having material success and peace of mind.

I had to go deeper than personal development. The next thing I started to explore was what I like to call, "The Land of Kumbaya!!"

It was time to seek the spiritual gurus, baby! I got on the spiritual bandwagon. I thought the tried-and-true spiritual practices would be the magic pill. Spoiler Alert: They weren't.

The truth is, to be peaceful, fearless, calm, and prosperous, you have to go BEYOND the mind. But, alas, it is a slippery slope. The charlatans, the false gurus, and the "freaks" are often widely respected in this field.

I believe my work as a sales and success coach gave me a huge advantage. Over the years I learned to measure everything. I applied this to my pursuit. As a self-proclaimed spiritual scientist, I put everything I learned to the test. As a result, I routinely tracked, monitored, and measured the activities and results I got from my various teachers.

I threw out what didn't work. I kept what worked. I measured new teachings against what I had learned in the past to see if I could improve my results.

I wanted peace. I wanted to have that big silly grin on my face no matter what was happening in my world. I was ruthless in my pursuit.

Unfortunately, I found most of the spiritual teachers and gurus were just re-purposing a version of "working on the mind," which led me right back to the Personal Development Prison. They weren't enlightened. They didn't have a quiet mind. They were selling peace of mind but didn't have it themselves.

If you want Quiet Mind Epic Life, then you have to let go of "working on the mind." It is a never-ending treadmill from hell which, unfortunately, leads right back to the Personal Development Prison.

If you are trying to master the mind, overcome the mind, change it, transform it, alter it, or train your mind, then you will never achieve a quiet mind.

Even more importantly, if you are trying to quiet the mind, then you are basically cutting the weeds off at the top. This book is about pulling the weeds out at the *roots* so that the mind's motive for thinking is eliminated altogether. Read that again. Let that sink in.

Discoveries From the Guru Parade

Here's what I've discovered.

If you want profound states of peace, then I'm sorry to break this to you, most meditation techniques won't work long-term.

Don't get me wrong, I've done a lot of meditation and I actually recommend it. But it's not the complete package. Meditation will only get temporary results. You can get the mind to go quiet while meditating and for a little while after you are done. But then the mind gets triggered and starts barraging you with unwanted chatter. You can't meditate all day and go to work or raise your kids. So it's not very practical.

Mindfulness is fairly effective but it's a long and hard road to a quiet mind. Staying mindful takes discipline because the mind is still motivated to talk. Unless you eliminate the minds motivation to talk, you will spend the rest of your life doing battle with the mind.

Affirmations don't quiet your mind. Chant an affirmation, and watch as the mind fights back and talks even more. You say, "I'm powerful" and the mind responds with, "If you are so powerful then why are you failing?"

Past life regressions don't quiet the mind. In fact, they give the mind more ammunition to judge and analyze things with a new, even more, irrelevant perspective. Suddenly the mind is saying things like, "Because I drowned in a past life, I have a fear of water" justifying another irrational fear that blocks you from doing something you would enjoy.

Silent retreats are wonderful and peaceful. Unfortunately, as soon as you get back into your regular life, the mind fires up its constant assault of unwanted commentary. The noise quickly returns.

New Age healing doesn't quiet the mind. I've tried and tried and tried as many healers as I could find. I've been to the "coo-coo house" and back. I am here to tell you quiet mind is not pervasive in the New Age movement.

You name it, I've probably done it. None of those modalities silenced my mind permanently. In fact, a bunch of them gave my mind even more ammunition to judge, assess and otherwise spew unwanted opinions at inopportune times.

Okay. You get it. I've got to stop myself now because I could list hundreds of things I tried that didn't permanently quiet the mind.

Let me say it like this...

Choose your mentors carefully. Look at the life they are living. Peace without practicality doesn't lead to an epic life. I've sat with some great masters and I've gone into incredible states of bliss. Unfortunately back at home, the mind rushed back in.

If you look more closely, you will see that most gurus and spiritual teachers have lives you wouldn't want to be living. Many are trapped by their own dogma, rules, and processes. Others are stuck in rituals they have been doing so long they no longer question it.

It's not all bad news. I got what I needed. I learned from many masters. Among the hundreds of gurus, teachers, healers, and practitioners were many true masters who provided me with valuable lessons and shared their enlightened consciousness with me.

I am forever grateful to Steven Sadlier, Dr. David Hawkins and Lane Lowry who each contributed to my Quiet Mind Epic Live in their own profound way. The actual list is way too long to list here.

This phase of my development was profound and invaluable to achieving my quiet mind.

The Spiritual Paradox: Being Powerful But Not Practical

To develop the process of achieving a quiet mind, I had to rise above the paradox that being spiritual was a powerful state but it wasn't very practical.

Let me set the stage. Here I am; successful but not satisfied. I'm positive, but I'm not peaceful. I realized that success wasn't what I was searching for. I wanted the pervasive sense of one-ness I had at age 9. I wanted that profound state of peace and to feel at one with all that is. Like I said before, "spiritual practice appeared to be the next natural step."

At first, I found refuge in an intensive meditation practice. I wanted to be in that peaceful place as much as possible. Initially, meditation provided me with that experience.

I devoured teachings on inner-consciousness looking for the secrets to inner peace. I sat with gurus. I studied the masters.

As a result, I began advancing again, and it was amazing. I was finally out of The Personal Development Prison. Meaning, the more I studied, the more peace and satisfaction I felt. Unlike The Personal Development Prison where the more I studied, the more dissatisfied I became with my life.

I found this new path profound and uplifting. I was geeking out on this spiritual enlightenment thing! As far as I could tell, this was the path to the promise land!!

I was learning how to transcend the mind.

For years, I was like a kid in a candy store.

Then, suddenly, there was another obstacle to overcome. There was another spiritual elephant in the room.

I hated to admit it, but I discovered that diving deeply into meditation and immersing oneself into the origins of consciousness, are devoid of any practical application.

I realized that all of the teachers and gurus who'd given me a piece of the puzzle had retreated from life and had become reclusive themselves. In other words, they'd bowed out of daily interaction with the world.

I found myself in the middle of a strange paradox.

How could a man like me living in Newport Beach, CA, working 60-80 hours a week, raising 4 kids, and juggling the demands of personal and professional success, attain advanced states of peace, calm, and fearlessness? How can I be a badass and be enlightened?

I couldn't simply follow those that had come before me. My teachers were living the life of a renunciate. By renouncing the world, they were not distracted by the demands of life. Very helpful when seeking to experience a quiet mind. Unfortunately, renunciation isn't practical for those of us living in modern society.

As a result, I ran smack dab into the unspoken paradox that no one was addressing: How to enter these enlightened states *and* be in the world.

I renewed my quest. My drive to attain the life I wanted was stronger than ever.

I refused to believe that in order to attain the advanced states of peace, calm and fearlessness I desired, that I had to either:

- renounce my worldly possessions and go into a reclusive state

  OR

- fail to live my life with the levels of peace, joy, and profound happiness I sought. Yuck!!

Then, the breakthrough happened.

I began to develop and apply a bizarre combination of modalities that started producing results.

Slowly, methodically, I was bolting together disciplines from my personal development days and fusing them with what I was doing on my spiritual path to enlightenment.

I applied this new cocktail of tools, techniques, processes, and strategies to my quest.

It worked.

Yes! I Am Experiencing Quiet Mind and My Life Is Epic

Years ago my mind went quiet. My fears disappeared. My worry and doubt disappeared. I was 9 years old again! Boom! I was experiencing pervasive sense of oneness, as I participated in normal life activities.

On the outside, I looked like the same old Matthew, but on the inside, it was like the door opened. It was as if I had stepped into a reality infinitely better than I could have imagined.

As a result, I do not experience fear unless the body is threatened by something in the environment, like avoiding an oncoming car.

I know this potentially sounds like an exaggeration. But there is no other way to say it. I don't worry about anything. I don't fret. I don't have fear anymore.

As a result, I am more creative than I have ever been in my life. My courage seems to be boundless. If I want to do something, I do it. I am not stopped in any way by my mind. I might be stopped by the world or the environment, but I am not stopped by irrational fears.

Having a quiet mind and experiencing enlightened states does not mean that I'm perfect. I still make dumb moves. I still screw things up. I fail. I still get triggered into degrading behaviors. I get imbalanced and overdose on sugar (my drug of choice these days). There are still many behaviors that I have not taken the time to transform.

That said, I am operating in an enlightened state. I know that the source of life within me is the source of life in everyone and everything else. We are all one thing expressing itself with infinite variety.

For example: With a shift in my mind I can experience profound states of ecstasy in my body. I look into a room and I can see the pervasive energy and information that is us, connecting us, creating us. Sometimes I stare to deeply into people's eyes and they tell me that I'm looking into their soul. People go into states of profound peace when we focus together. It's amazing, and it's nuts.

That's some of the weirdo stuff. But it's also very practical. For example I don't worry about my goals coming to fruition.

In fact, I have a completely different experience of my goals these days. My goals present themselves as possibilities, and then they just start happening. I enjoy the process of helping them come into the world. It's fun. There's no stress about it.

I'm practical. Some goals happen. Some don't. I don't have any attachment either way. My goals are a form of entertainment, not necessities that determine my happiness or success. This is distinct because I used to fret and obsess over my goals. I used to suffer the whole time until I accomplished the goal. Now I just enjoy the process.

Because I feel connected to a universal oneness. Because I am feeling connected to all things. I have astonishing levels of courage. I am not attached to the outcome. So I just go for it and see what happens. As a result of this detachment, I have achieved many great feats in my life. This is the state I call Enlightened Prosperity.

> Enlightenment provides you with a context to enjoy unbelievable freedom, creativity, power, and influence over your life. As you transcend cultural conditioning, limiting dogma and unexamined beliefs you will have more power over your life. When you see life as innocent, perfect, or meaningless, you deal with things much more sensibly.

I've started many companies. I have several profitable ventures today. I've made tens of millions of dollars. I've written books. I go after my dreams. I have always wanted to be a rockstar so I released several music albums. I didn't become an actual rockstar but I took action without fear and enjoyed the process.

I won't bore you with a list my accomplishments. At the time of this writing, I am a 50-year-old man with a lot of battle scars and a lot of victories.

Here's my point. Having a quiet mind, living with Enlightened Perspectives and being fearless is unbelievably practical.

I highly recommend it.

Chapter 3
The Power of Enlightenment

"Being enlightened is just a perspective."

Enlightenment is not a place. It's not a destination. It's a state. It's a point of view. It's a contextual framework.

Each enlightened person will behave differently than all other enlightened people. You won't do it the way I do it. I won't do it the way you do it. There is no one right way or wrong way to be enlightened. Why?

Because enlightenment is just a perspective about existence. Here are some of the definitions from Merriam-Webster Dictionary to help put this idea into context.

Merriam-Webster's Definition of "Enlightened":

- Freed from ignorance and misinformation

- Having or showing a good understanding of how people should be treated: not ignorant or narrow in thinking

Merriam-Webster's Definition of "Enlightenment":

- The state of having knowledge or understanding

- A final spiritual state marked by the absence of desire or suffering

I know, I know. You may be thinking, "Isn't this an Eastern religious thing Matthew?" That's what I thought at first too. But, truthfully, enlightenment is not a religious thing at all. It's a people thing. It's a word that spiritual teachers, healers, and religious philosophers have used to describe the ultimate human condition.

Enlightenment Redefined for Today

Here's *my* definition of enlightenment.

> *Enlightenment is the recognition that the source of life within you is the source of life in everyone and everything else. We are all one thing expressing itself with infinite variety.*

This gives you...

- The ability to see what has been hidden by the contextual filters of the survival mind
- The ability to accept what you see without unwanted emotion or reaction
- The freedom to act in accordance with your true desires
- The ability to operate completely free from guilt, obligation, cultural dogma, societal programming, fear, concern, doubt, and worry

Enlightenment gives you the mind-bending power to create your epic life. At the center of my definition of enlightenment, is the ability to accept what you see without unwanted emotion or reaction.

The more you accept, the less you resist. The less you resist, the happier you are. The happier you are, the easier it is to think, express, and create the life you want.

Happiness is one of the cornerstone experiences of being enlightened.

When you are happy, you are more resourceful. You are also easier to deal with. Moreover, enlightenment gives you an unbelievably strategic advantage in your life. Success in all aspects of life is much easier when you are happy.

Now don't make the mistake that just because you are happy you are also effective. Happiness and effectiveness are two different things.

Being enlightened gives you the ability to be happy regardless of the circumstances. This simply means that your ability to be effective is enhanced because you are not in a state of resistance. It doesn't *make* you effective. It allows you to accept the challenges you face when working to become effective at something.

Enlightenment unlocks courage by recontextualizing what you fear. With the release of fear, you have a surge of creative energy. Backburner projects become front-burner projects. New projects mean new challenges to overcome. An Enlightened Perspective creates an empowering context that allows you to fearlessly embrace the challenges and overcome them.

As you overcome challenges, in essence, you become more effective. Therefore, enlightenment is a very powerful tool for becoming effective at the things in which you are interested.

This is a state of unbelievable freedom, creativity, power, and influence over your life. As you pierce through the veil of the mind's denial system, you begin to see life as innocent, perfect, and meaningless. This power allows you to deal with things very sensibly. There is no suffering. There is no desire. There is no worry. There is no doubt. There is just bold creative energy.

When you become enlightened, there is inspiration. There is compassion. There is a level of joy that feels so good you can't put it into words.

So how do you get there?

Modern Enlightenment: 6 Qualities of Being Enlightened

In the end, I can sum up the experience of being enlightened in six qualities.

1: Wisdom

When you achieve your enlightened state (and you will), you are going to be flooded with information that was previously blocked by your mind's fears, concerns, and distortions.

It's like the curtains are open and suddenly you see the world for the first time. The world just makes sense to you. People no longer surprise you. Your curiosity explodes within you. You will feel like you are the character in the movie *Limitless* who takes the drug, and suddenly he is using 100% of his brain's capacity.

Initially, it will surprise the people around you, and they will react by saying, "How did you know that?" The truth is, you won't be able to explain it.

Enlightenment is a state where more and more of life just makes sense and seems obvious. With practice, it gets stronger and stronger.

2: Profound peace

In an enlightened state, you are no longer limited by the perceptual filters created by the mind. You will no longer be burdened by your mind's biological drive to survive.

Consequently, concerns about success, relationships, money, your future, and even your children will disappear. You will see the beauty in everything. You will see the perfection in all situations and the inter-connectivity of all things.

Because of this awareness, you will feel profoundly, deeply, and indescribably at home in your own skin.

When you achieve your enlightened state, you will know with certainty that there is nowhere to go. Nothing to do. Nothing to accomplish. Nothing to apologize for. No one to impress. No mind chatter dictating orders, mandating the completion of to-do lists, and no more worrying about the future. This is *true* freedom. You will be free from the bondage of the mind.

Peace is pervasive, persistent, and frankly...awesome! It's a highly recommended state! I can't wait for you to join me here.

3: Fear disappears

When you are enlightened, you have a distinct absence of fear. You are not careless or irrational but quite the opposite. You are more rational then you have ever been before.

This fearlessness stems from being present to your infinite nature. You see no ending and no beginning. You see the pervasive energetic quality of your existence. There is nothing to be afraid of. All of life's concerns seem like comedy. You find yourself giggling and giddy on a regular basis.

Death seems natural. Death even seems interesting. For me, I'm personally curious if my insights about death are correct. I'm not afraid of it. I'm fascinated by life and death. You will have your own version of this perspective. From this perspective, fear will disappear as a mental function.

Fear will still be there as a bodily function to keep you out of danger, that is, when actual physical danger is present. If there is a lion in your living room, thankfully fear will take over and your body will naturally react.

The irrational fears about getting a promotion, the "What if I don't make enough money?", "Will my kids go to college?", "Am I pretty?", "Will I spend my life alone?", etc. etc. will all disappear.

4: Courage

When you achieve your enlightened state, you will experience the absence of fear and the presence of trust and inner knowing. In other words, the world will just make sense. Gone are the days of being perplexed. Gone are the days of fretting over what *might* happen.

The result of enlightenment is an absurd level of courage. I say absurd because the wildest, craziest ideas that lie dormant in your consciousness will make their way to your actual to-do list. Plans you once thought too big, too crazy, too out of your reach, suddenly become real possibilities.

5: Your presence is experienced as a gift

Another way of saying that you are enlightened is to say that you are a high-conscious person. Consciousness is both what you are aware of and what you accept. The more aware you are and the more you accept what you are aware of, the higher your consciousness level.

When you are a high-conscious person, you can see much, much more than the average person. You see between the lines.

You see the program is actually running the people. You see the imbalances in people's perceptions. In other words, you have an expansive awareness of the world around you. You have wisdom that you can't explain to others.

On the other hand, a high-conscious person doesn't just see more than other people. When you are a high-conscious person, you are able to accept what you see.

What is imbalanced becomes balanced around you. Your presence creates greater levels of order and integrity in people and in the environment. Everything seems easy, effortless, and flowing in your presence.

6: You are special because you realize that you aren't special

In your enlightened state, there's no judgment. There's no opinion. Positions like better, worse, good, and bad all disappear. It becomes apparent that judgments and opinions are survival tools that aren't relevant any longer.

Everyone is celebrated. All human experiences are revered and appreciated. Clearly, you have the discernment to recognize that you are experiencing the world differently than others. From an infinite perspective, this enlightened state feels like one of an infinite number of potential states you could experience here on Earth.

Everyone is different. But there *will* be some version of these insights for you.

When the door of enlightenment is opened, you have an unwavering feeling that you have come to Earth many times. Even if you are a Christian or don't believe in reincarnation, you will feel something like this. It is experienced as a great relief and puts an end to the majority of the suffering you have experienced.

In your enlightened state, you don't feel any self-importance. You don't feel better than anyone.

You see yourself as a part of the whole. No singular part of the system is more important than the other

On my journey to a quiet mind, I have tried many things. Some worked. Some didn't. Some created the conditions for enlightened consciousness to flow through me. Other methods were a waste of time.

The following chapters are what worked for me.

Over the last decade, I've used these ideas, processes, and techniques to assist my friends, family, private coaching clients, and private mastermind clients to achieve Rapid Enlightenment.

Now, it's your turn.

Chapter 4
The Rapid Enlightenment Process Explained

Are you ready? Let's go.

The Rapid Enlightenment Process helps you create a state of everlasting peace where worry and fear become irrelevant.

The Rapid Enlightenment Process helps you rise above cultural conditioning, limiting dogma and unexamined beliefs.

The Rapid Enlightenment Process helps you see that all is well in the world. There is nothing to resist or push against.

The Rapid Enlightenment Process causes you to adopt Enlightened Perspectives which produce the sense that all is well, regardless of the circumstances you find yourself in.

From an Enlightened Perspective, the positions of the ego are abandoned. You are free to experience and express whatever uplifts and inspires you.

From an Enlightened Perspective, suffering is transcended as you realize nothing needs to be changed, altered or avoided.

From an Enlightened Perspective, the world is whole and complete exactly as it is. Urgency is replaced by a deep connection to your infinite nature.

As a result, accomplishment becomes effortless. Peace of mind is pervasive.

I call this Enlightened Prosperity.

The word Enlightened has its origin in the Middle English word "inlihtan" or "to shine"

The word Prosperity has its origin in the Latin word "prosperus" or "doing well."

When experiencing Enlightened Prosperity your essence is shining through cultural conditioning, limiting dogma and unexamined beliefs AND you are doing well personally, professionally, mentally, spiritually, financially. Everything is working. You are unlimited. You are free.

The only thing between you and the Enlightened Prosperity you seek is limiting dogma.

Limiting dogma creates a paradigm that places an arbitrary ceiling on your happiness, your success, and your self-expression.

I'll say it like this: There is no way to prove if your beliefs about yourself and the world are true. But... You still believe them. You defend your positions, points of view and perspectives like they are important for the well-being of the species. Sometimes you even act like your life depends on them.

In a nutshell, you are following rules that don't exist.

- You are living via beliefs that limit you.

- You defend perspectives that are a figment of your imagination.

- You diminish yourself because you don't meet arbitrary standards

- You feeling bad because you don't measure up.

Cultural conditioning, limiting dogma and unexamined beliefs arc the tethers holding you back from ascending into enlightened states. They literally block you from the recognition that the source of life within you is the source of life in everyone and everything else. We are all one thing expressing itself with infinite variety.

The Rapid Enlightenment Process is a series of contextual shifts that destroy cultural conditioning, limiting dogma and unexamined beliefs and replaces them with new enlightened dogma aka Enlightened Perspectives.

As I like to say "if you are going to make things up, why not make things up that feel good?"

The Rapid Enlightenment Process recontextualizes the fundamental questions about the meaning of life, and your role in it while striving to create the most empowering context possible.

Meaning, the Rapid Enlightenment Process exposes you to a new set of contexts that naturally cause you to move away from survival mind and into quiet mind, from limiting dogma to enlightened dogma.

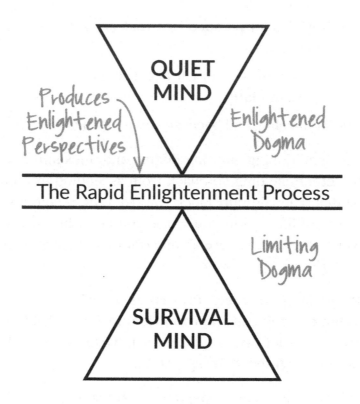

The Rapid Enlighenment Process produces Enlightened Perspectives.

Years ago Kristen was having dinner with a group of people she met at a personal development seminar. At the end of the meal, someone offered to pick up the check and treat everyone to dinner. One woman said, "thank you so much! I have a track record for getting things for free!" Kristen's eye turned the size of quarters. "Wow," she thought. "Now there's an awesome context to live inside." Yep, that's some effective dogma in action.

Look, I know you were born predisposed to unique perspectives and behaviors. But you don't know how you got this way.

- You aren't like your brothers and sisters.
- You see things differently than your parents.
- You were born with irrational fears, and you know it.
- You like chocolate, others like vanilla.
- You have no idea where these propensities and preferences come from.

To really illustrate my point, let me give you some examples of cultural conditioning, limiting dogma and unexamined beliefs to consider. To keep it short, I'll refer to it all as dogma.

Cultural dogma

- Men work and women raise the babies
- Get a job - start a family - save for retirement
- You have to put the kid's needs above your own
- Find a good man who can take care of you
- You need to marry to validate you are a good man

Religious dogma

- Follow the rules in the books
- God is judging you
- God will be offended if you say the wrong thing
- I have to tithe

- I have to recite incantations
- Heaven and hell exist

Sexual dogma

- Sex is dirty
- Sex is sacred
- Sex is private
- Sex is only for married people

Atheist dogma

- There is no god
- There is no purpose to life
- Birth, life, and death are completely random
- My actions have no impact on the greater whole

Success dogma

- I have to get a college degree
- When I accomplish X I can stop working
- The more I achieve, the happier I will be
- Successful people had to compromise their values to get ahead
- My family is successful, so I have to be
- I don't have the same advantages as other people

Money dogma

- Money is bad
- Money is good
- I have to save money
- I have to give to charity
- Rich people are unethical
- Poor people are lazy
- My value is determined by my bank account
- I have to make a certain amount each year in order to feel accomplished

Physical body dogma

- I have to work out in order to stay healthy
- Pampering yourself is a luxury
- Others thrive on little sleep
- I have to get up early in order to be successful

Over time, each of us accidentally adopts a set of dogma, or beliefs about the world, and then fill in the gaps with guesses about what's really going on. Some of it is cultural, some gender-based, some is familial. The origin doesn't matter.

In the end, you can't answer life's fundamental questions but that doesn't stop you from making up a story and defending it like you know the answers.

As human beings we seem to be hard-wired to develop stories about the meaning of life, how to live, what happens when we die, what it means to be a good person, etc.

Whatever version we adopt isn't the "truth," it's dogma.

> *Limiting dogma is what blocks you from experiencing a quiet mind.*

The Rapid Enlightenment Process is a series of contextual shifts that destroy cultural conditioning, limiting dogma and unexamined beliefs and replaces them with new enlightened dogma aka Enlightened Perspectives.

In a nutshell, it moves you from survival mind to quiet mind.

There are four components of The Rapid Enlightenment Process

1. Seeing the mind as a survival mechanism: The Drunk Monkey. (*Chapter 5*)

2. Understanding what causes The Drunk Monkey to talk: The Hidden Motives To Survive. (*Chapter 6*)

3. Transcending the mind's limiting dogma: Recontextualization. (*Chapter 7*)

4. Piercing through the veil of the denial mechanism: Muscle testing. (*Chapter 8*)

When you recontextualize the fundamental questions about the meaning of life and your role in it, you naturally being to create an empowering context. When you are living in an empowering context, you move out of a survival context and the mind begins to quiet.

This is why no amount of self-help, or personal development aimed to master the mind, overcome the mind, change it, transform it, alter it, or train your mind, will ever produce a quiet mind state.

You must transcend the mind. To do that, you must eliminate its purpose for talking in the first place.

That's what we are about to do.

In the coming chapters, I am going to take you step-by-step through each component of the Rapid Enlightenment Process, and then share proven Enlightened Perspectives that will cause your mind to go quiet.

Let's begin.

Chapter 5
Meet The Drunk Monkey

"The Drunk Monkey is the mouthpiece of the survival mind."

The Drunk Monkey is a nickname I created to describe that part of the mind responsible for the incessant, non-stop commentary that robs your peace of mind and blocks you from experiencing a quiet mind.

••••••••••••••••••••••••••••••••••••

The Drunk Monkey is great for survival, but as you are about to discover, it's terrible at thriving.

••••••••••••••••••••••••••••••••••••

Yes, I know "drunk monkey" is grammatically incorrect. You see, in 1991 I was in my 20s partying like a rock star and conversely I was deeply immersed in personal development work.

When the concept of the Monkey Mind was introduced to me by Jose Silva, creator of The Silva Method, I thought to myself "If the mind is like a monkey, then my mind is like a drunk monkey."

I began using this metaphor in my coaching practice and the name stuck.

You may have heard it called "The Lizard Brain". Whatever the label, this animal biology has a very legitimate job: to keep you safe and to keep you alive. It does that by making sure you maintain the status quo.

Status Quo is Latin meaning "the state in which." The modern definition is "the existing state of affairs, especially regarding social or political issues." In simple terms, status quo means "how things are" or "common beliefs held by the mainstream."

You are about to become distinctly aware that The Drunk Monkey is great for survival, but it's terrible at thriving. The Drunk Monkey LOVES the status quo because is to known. It's easy to identify, and therefore its safe.

Unfortunately the status quo of your life - how things are - will be challenged as you seek to quiet the mind. This in itself is a major threat to The Drunk Monkey.

In fact, in order to live in an enlightened state, you must transcend the survival mind. You must see that The Drunk Monkey is purely biological. This allows you to step back from your life and examine if feeling stressed, anxious, overwhelmed, or any other negative feeling is really necessary at all.

Of course, you always discover that negativity in any of its forms is not actually necessary. When we are experiencing joy, it is much easier to handle day-to-day challenges. When we have peace of mind, our sense of well-being increases and our creativity explodes. Effectiveness, resourcefulness, ease, and flow are all indicators you are thriving. They are natural outcomes when you adopt the context that we are all one thing expressing with infinite variety.

Awareness of The Drunk Monkey allows you to confront complex situations and easily conquer them. When you have the ability to see The Drunk Monkey rambling and reacting to this and that, you start to see the situation from a different perspective and you are able to respond in an effective manner. You know that all is well, and you respond accordingly.

Effectiveness, resourcefulness, ease and flow do not exist in the domain of The Drunk Monkey. The Drunk Monkey is the mouthpiece of the survival mind.

Ultimately, as you continue to engage The Rapid Enlightenment Process, The Drunk Monkey's motives for talking will fade away. It will stop talking to you, and you will transition into a state of pervasive oneness filled with wonder and joy. You will experience the peace that comes with a quiet mind.

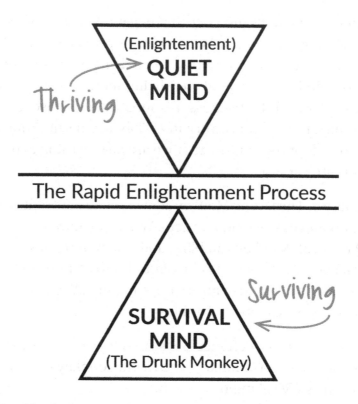

The Rapid Enlightenment Process moves you from surviving to thriving.

How did The Drunk Monkey get so much control?

The mistake we all make is believing that we are The Drunk Monkey. Oops! You are not the thinking in your head. Let me prove it.

Have you noticed that you can't control the talking in your head most of the time? The Drunk Monkey rambles and reacts to things whether you want it to or not. It talks without permission. It interrupts.

Here's the game-changer context to adopt: You are the one listening to the talking in your head. You are NOT the one doing the talking.

It isn't you. You are the witness of the thoughts. Thoughts happen whether you participate or not. You know this because you see that trying to control thoughts is nearly impossible. Sometimes you can do it during prolonged periods of concentration or meditation, but soon you are interrupted by the survival mind.

When the survival mind is running the show you take action based on misinformation and illusions.

The Drunk Monkey in your head leads to endless frustration and negativity when you believe that you are the thinker of the thoughts.

> This is the #1 problem with self-help, and the reason people get stuck in The Personal Development Prison. When you inaccurately believe that you are your thoughts, you believe that your mind can be dominated with positivity. You seek to control the biological nature of thinking in an effort to experience more joy. That's like using a car engine to brew a pot of coffee.

> Using the survival mind in an attempt to experience peace of mind, is well, illogical. Yet, you and I have spent years on this path. It stops here. Today is the day you release trying to

"change your thinking to change your life" and you begin to transcend the survival mind altogether.

Thinking is merely a biological function. It's just brain chemistry. Thinking is just energy moving through the neurons in your brain. You are not The Drunk Monkey, just like you are not your body. You are the one observing your body.

Think about it like this: Do you beat your heart? Do you maintain your balance? Do you digest food? No, you don't. These are automatic biological functions. On examination, you'll begin to see that thinking is also biological.

Slow down for just a second and ponder this thought: your body operates independently of you. It is doing what it is doing without your input.

Your mind, The Drunk Monkey, is also a part of your biology. In other words, it operates independently of you as well. Have you ever laid down at night wishing that your mind would stop talking so you can go to sleep? That's The Drunk Monkey doing its job. Planning, ruminating, forecasting, strategizing, replaying, lamenting, and problem-solving. It's thinking whether you want it to or not.

The Drunk Monkey is not designed for enlightenment. It's not designed to recognize all is well. It has no use for the idea that we are all one thing expressing with infinite variety.

You are committed to thriving. You don't seek Quiet Mind Epic Life because you are in a survival state.

Joy, peace, happiness, satisfaction, prosperity, love, and contentment are not survival pursuits. They are the pursuits of a person who is thriving.

The message is plain and simple: the talking in your head is a non-stop survival machine that is relatively useless if you want to live with a quiet mind.

Awareness makes you flexible, which reveals new options and gives you power. Awareness of The Drunk Monkey is empowering. The more you see The Drunk Monkey at work in your life, the less purpose it has and more epic your life will become.

The Drunk Monkey In Action

Here are some basic descriptions to help you see The Drunk Monkey in action.

The Drunk Monkey talks you out of taking action on the things that are most important to you. As you will discover later, The Drunk Money believes that it's psychic and can predict the future. On examination, you'll see this just one sneaky survival tactic called Unconscious Reflexes that The Drunk Monkey uses against you. I take you on a deep dive into the Unconscious Reflexes of The Drunk Monkey later in the book.

The Drunk Monkey is your anti-cheerleader. It makes fun of you. It mentally abuses you. It calls you names. It tells you that you can't do things. It tells you that your ideas won't work.

The Drunk Monkey distracts you with the unimportant. It uses the latest episode of your favorite show to distract you from doing what you promised you would do. It encourages you to web surf or engage in social media instead of working on things you want to do that move your goals and dreams forward.

What you want, your deepest desires, your creative pursuits, your goals - they all threaten the status quo.

Because The Drunk Monkey is survival based, it fears change. Change represents a threat to what is known. If you try to break from the pack and do what inspires you, then The Drunk Monkey will use its mental and emotional tools to bring you back to status quo.

The Drunk Monkey's tools are very familiar to you. To put it in a word, these tools represent "Negativity".

Here's a list of survival based emotions to help you understand when The Drunk Monkey is running the show:

- Fear
- Doubt
- Worry
- Anxiety
- Bitterness
- Agitation
- Condemnation
- Agony

- Crankiness
- Loneliness
- Defeat
- Animosity
- Discouragement
- Grimness
- Humiliation
- Impatience
- Crushed
- Pissed off

You get the picture, right? The Drunk Monkey's job is to motivate you to avoid harm and seek safety and homeostasis. That means you will survive longer. Anything other than a quiet mind is just The Drunk Monkey doing its thing. Remember, thriving is NOT the domain of The Drunk Monkey.

To achieve Quiet Mind Epic Life, you must be able to notice The Drunk Monkey using its tools to motivate you. Awareness is critical. After you trigger awareness, you must practice seeing the situation as it is, rather than being blinded by the biological motives of The Drunk Monkey.

That said, understanding the functionality of The Drunk Monkey is just the beginning. Now we are going to dive into what fuels the survival mind. That's where The Hidden Motives To Survive come in.

Chapter 6
Hidden Motives To Survive

The Hidden Motives To Survive create the illusion that strategizing, lamenting, and prophesying will produce a quiet mind state. They won't.

The Hidden Motives To Survive have been programmed into human consciousness for millennia. And, they work, for living a survival based existence. For someone like you, whose basic needs are already met, using these motives to survive is extremely degrading and they block your path to experiencing enlightened states.

Each Hidden Motive To Survive is an invisible energy field that is pervasive throughout human consciousness. It's in your soul. It's in your personality. It's in your aura. It's in your chakras. It's in your DNA.

These memories are traditionally called Karma. You might not be familiar with the exact meaning of that word. Here's what Google dictionary says, "Karma is the sum of a person's actions in this and previous states of existence; deciding their fate in future existences."

Karma is literally the memory of your soul in this lifetime and in "previous states of existence".

Karma influences everything you do. It creates a filter that distorts the way you see things. When you see things differently, you behave differently.

Let me ask you a question. Have you ever encountered someone who gets defensive for no reason?

As a high-conscious person, you can step back and see that a defensive person has most likely felt treated unfairly in the past. It's part of their memory. Now, they are interacting with you and they are afraid they will be treated unfairly.

In essence, they are afraid they will be treated poorly in the future, and it makes them defensive in the present. As a result, they react to non-defensive situations in an inappropriately defensive way. That imaginary fear actually causes them to be treated unfairly over and over again.

That is Karma in its most basic manifestation.

The Hidden Motives To Survive are an expression of Karma. The motives live in our individual consciousness and, more importantly, they live in our collective consciousness.

Think of The Hidden Motives To Survive as basic parts or building blocks of survival consciousness. They are pervasive. The Hidden Motives To Survive are to survival consciousness what the Periodic Table of Elements are to the physical world.

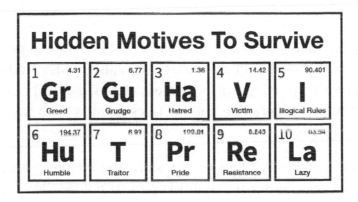

The ten Hidden Motives To Survive are the building blocks of survival consciousness.

The Drunk Monkey is fueled by these Hidden Motives To Survive. The Drunk Monkey is an ingrained set of habitual thought processes that evolved over millennia as a way to stay alive longer. It is the mouthpiece of the survival mind.

While we have discussed extensively the familial, social, cultural and environmental conditioning at the heart of The Drunk Monkey, it is only the tip of the iceberg.

Now it's time to go deeper.

Seeing The Hidden Motives To Survive Gives You An Advantage

As I've mentioned before, when my mind went silent back in 2006, there was an experience of overwhelming joy. Now I want to share with you the deeply perplexing new set of awareness that came with it.

In a quiet mind state, I was present to the beauty and grandeur of life, people, and circumstances. I was also confronted by the awareness of greed, grudges, hatred, victim, illogical rules, and a host of other degrading perspectives coming from the people I interacted with.

It was like suddenly I had x-ray vision, and I could see into the fabric of consciousness itself. I began to notice the quality of consciousness of people. I saw a set of contexts and paradigms they were living inside of.

When you are not distracted by the mind and its incessant planning, ruminating, forecasting, strategizing, replaying, lamenting, and problem-solving you begin to notice a very subtle energy emanating from other people.

It's like people are little radio stations transmitting their unique combo-pack of Hidden Motives To Survive.

> *Seeing the Hidden Motives To Survive gives you an enormous advantage in life. For example, when you can see someone who is being influenced by the Hidden Motive Pride you can begin to see things from their perspective and have compassion that they are doing their best given the context they are operating inside of.*

Over time, it became apparent that these motives to survive are pervasive throughout consciousness. When a motive was present, it would trigger The Drunk Monkey.

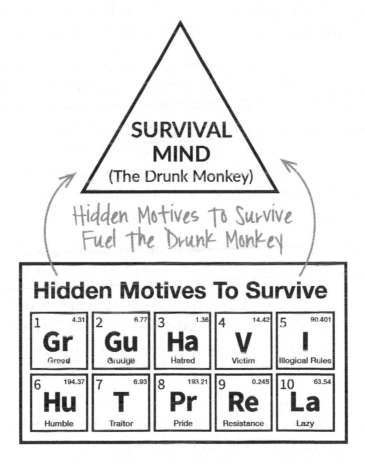

The Hidden Motives To Survive act as the fuel that gets The Drunk Monkey fired up, and spewing its concerns, worries, and fears.

The Drunk Monkey is the Effect, Not The Cause, of Mental Disturbance

Let me step back and share how this revealed itself to me in my journey as both the devotee seeking enlightened states and the guy hired to teach others to have happiness and success.

In 1989, at the beginning of my personal development studies, I was concerned with feeling better and becoming empowered by changing my emotions. I used affirmation, visualizations, and things like Neuro-Linguistic Programming (NLP) to manipulate my nervous system and get myself to respond to lives challenges in a more effective way. Standing up, rapid breathing, beating my chest, and reciting affirmations changed my state temporarily, but not permanently.

To create a permanent change in my response to life, I had to rise above manipulating my body and address my emotions.

As I evolved, I realized that the nervous system was triggering my emotions in an effort to evoke some action. I realized that emotions are a biological system to get you moving one way or another.

"Hmm," I contemplated, "How do I get the emotions under control so I'm not so reactive?" I began to realize that my nervous system was influenced by my psychology.

How I saw something either created a moving towards or moving away response. So I moved from emotional control to mental control.

As a result, I stopped trying to tweak my nervous system by beating my chest and started working on my context.

Much of what I'm teaching you in this book came from those studies, my realizations, and the results I achieved in that phase of my development.

Over the years, I became masterful at being able to control The Drunk Monkey. I would discipline my thoughts. I would bust The Drunk Monkey and tell it to shut up. I would try to repress it and tell it that I was the one in control.

Yet, there seemed to be something underneath The Drunk Monkey that triggered it, whether I was in control or not.

Try as I might to keep myself in a good state, my mind would periodically go berserk. I would be overwhelmed with sadness. Yet, my life was amazing.

Out of nowhere I would feel powerless and get angry. Angry at myself. Angry at the world for being a bad place. Angry at family and friends for not doing what I wanted them to do.

When I was in these degraded states, I made really bad decisions on a regular basis. Decisions that produced results contrary to what I wanted.

I was consistently blinded by greed. I would become afraid that there wasn't going to be enough business, money, clients, or opportunity. It drove me to be reactive rather than strategic.

I could control my body. I could control my emotions. I could control my mind. I had those skills and techniques down. Yet, something kept knocking me off track.

Through my meditation, help from mentors, thousands of hours of coaching calls with clients, and the emergence of my quiet mind, it became clear that The Drunk Monkey is an effect of something else. Something deeper. Something more pervasive.

Enter the Hidden Motives To Survive: Non-local aspects of consciousness that are part of your soul's memory known as Karma.

Have you ever met someone whose presence instantly made you feel annoyed? Consider the idea that they triggered the presence of grudge or hatred inside of you.

Have you ever noticed that watching the news creates a feeling of powerlessness? The purpose of the news is to activate victim in our collective and individual consciousness.

Have you done tons of work to forgive your parents, and yet, they still trigger you into negativity? Why?

When The Hidden Motives To Survive are present, they act like a tuning fork. Ding. "Hatred" gets triggered in someone over there, and dong, Hatred gets triggercd in you. You get triggered by the information that someone emits or represents and without warning, that energy awakens memories in your soul that have been a part of your survival system.

In a nutshell, a motive to survive was being triggered, and you were powerless to do anything about it. All the training in the world can't help you in that moment. You are like a train that has too much momentum to stop.

The Hidden Motives to Survive are not a part of personal development. You can't go to a traditional self-help seminar and learn about them. They aren't dealt with in religious settings. They don't get addressed in new age or spiritual studies.

Yet, if you want to experience a quiet mind, if you want to go into enlightened states, you MUST understand the role the Hidden Motives To Survive play in the process.

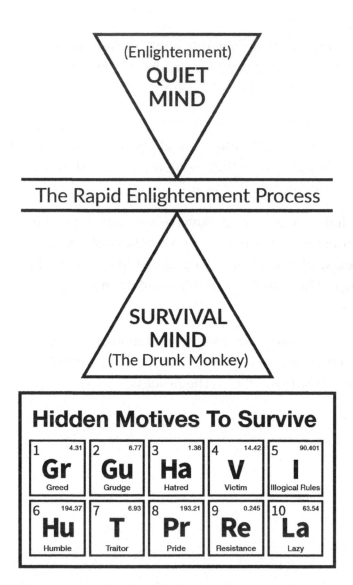

The Hidden Motives To Survive fuel The Drunk Monkey, the mouthpiece of the survival mind. The Rapid Enlightenment Process produces Enlightened Perspectives that natually cause you to experience a quiet mind state.

Here's a list of the Hidden Motives to Survive that are most likely degrading your experience at varying degrees right now.

Which ones immediately jump out at you?

1. **Pride** - Often experienced as arrogance. Trying to be more important and prove you are above others. Overly attached to being right about things. Trying to look smarter than others. The quality of having an excessively high opinion of oneself or one's importance.

2. **Greed** - The fear that there won't be enough opportunity, time, money, food, or resources. The intense and selfish desire for something for fear of not having enough.

3. **Victim** - Feeling powerless as if life is out of your control.

4. **Illogical Rules** - Unconsciously following rules that degrade you. Believing that these rules are appropriate, important, or valuable even though, with examination they aren't real and they make your life worse.

5. **Humble** - Having or showing a modest or low estimate of one's own importance. Making yourself less than.

6. **Traitor** - Hiding your true feelings or thoughts for fear of losing a benefit.

7. **Lazy** - Avoiding hard things in an effort to keep a benefit. Avoiding activity or exertion: not energetic or vigorous.

8. **Resistance** - Pushing against ideas, activities and people in an effort to protect against the loss of a benefit. The fear of a negative future.

9. **Hatred** - Intense dislike or ill will. Fear of differences. Broken expectations that turn into anger.

10. **Grudge** - Holding onto a persistent feeling of ill will or resentment to make sure bad things won't happen.

I suspect that one or more jumped out at you. Here's the bad news. You are currently being affected by the energy of all 10.

These Hidden Motives are pervasive throughout human consciousness. They are the driving energy behind 90% or more of your decisions. Your relationships, where you live, who you live with, your job, your hobbies, your drive for inner peace, it's all being driven by Hidden Motives to Survive.

Unfortunately, you and I are going to have to deal with one of the worst betrayals of all. Your drive to be enlightened is actually being driven by a Hidden Motive To Survive. The Drunk Monkey actually believes that being enlightened is a very good survival strategy. Even that will have to be transcended.

The motives aren't active all the time. You have one that is a theme for your life. My theme is Greed. Kristen's is Traitor.

On reflection, I see that in the past I have been unconsciously motivated to gather as many resources as I can for fear that there won't be enough. Consequently, I have made millions of dollars, collected piles of stuff and have stockpiles of things "we might need" if there is an emergency.

You might think, "Sounds dreamy, Matthew! I want lots of money and lots of stuff too!" But that's only the illusion you are attracted to. The ice cream on top of the cow pie.

The dark ugly truth is that greed has created self-fulfilling prophecies in my life over and over again. Because of my irrational fears about money, I've made terrible financial decisions that have put my family in debilitating debt. Greed has blinded me to the downside of overextending our lifestyle. Rather than seeking the peace I wanted, greed drove me to buy things to look good and spend money rather than invest money in assets that build our wealth.

At the time of this writing, you are getting me five years into the transformation that has occurred because of the discovery of the Hidden Motives. By eradicating the karma of greed in my consciousness, I've finally turned the ship in a new direction of financial integrity vs.. the financial gluttony of greed.

And, I'm not ashamed to talk about it. If you want Quiet Mind Epic Life, then you have to look yourself in the mirror and admit that you have a sewer underneath your rose garden.

You'll soon discover when one or more of the Hidden Motives To Survive are activated in your consciousness, you will malfunction. You will not be in an effective state. Your life stops working well. When life isn't working, you get an indicator; you don't feel happy, lit up, and energized. When your personal system is compromised by the Hidden Motives, you don't feel right.

As you continue to train yourself in my methodology, you will get tipped off that a Hidden Motive is present because The Drunk Monkey engages an Unconscious Reflex like Forecasting The Negative. In the coming chapters, I take you through six Unconscious Reflexes of The Drunk Monkey so you can use awareness to mitigate their impact.

There will be stages to your Quiet Mind Epic Life journey. For example The Drunk Monkey is much easier to see than the Hidden Motives that drive it. Awareness of The Drunk Monkey may be your total focus for a while.

Over the years, I've seen that the ability to correct the imbalances of the Hidden Motives to Survive often take an outside source, like me, to help you see them and ultimately eradicate them.

Ultimately, together, we are updating the incorrect information in your soul with new up-to-date information.

It's like your computer. You don't see the underlying software running the show. You just see the result of the software based on the way you interact with it.

The Drunk Monkey is like the various buttons you can press in your program. Hidden Motives are the underlying code that makes the button appear and cause it to do something when you press it.

Each Hidden Motive To Survive is unconscious. It's literally driving you. It is like a filter. You are blind to it. You can't even sec the light it is blocking. You are like a person who has needed glasses but didn't know. When you start wearing glasses, you are dumbstruck by everything you had been missing.

This is about to happen to you with every aspect of your life.

Your eyes are about to be opened.

Chapter 7

Transcending The Mind's Limiting Dogma: Recontextualization

Recontextualization is the skill of describing conditions and circumstances in a way that creates an empowering reality for you.

This is a master skill. Initially, learning to Recontextualize will create the conditions for you to become enlightened. Then it will become a cornerstone tool to remain enlightened.

The world you live in creates the conditions for suffering and negativity. To achieve Quite Mind Epic Life, you must use Recontextualization to rise above suffering.

I'm going to teach you to transform your agitation into celebration. With this skill, you will become satisfied with what used to be unsatisfying.

Let me restate the benefit of learning to Recontextualize so you get it. No more suffering. No more agitation. No more dissatisfaction.

How does that sound?

If you are as devoted to being enlightened like I am, then you will practice Recontextualization for the rest of your life. This chapter will likely be something you read over and over again to let the nuances really sink in.

Let's review my definition of Enlightenment:

> *"Enlightenment is the recognition that the source of life within you is also the source of life in everyone and everything else. We are all one thing expressing itself with infinite variety."*

Now, let's smash through some of the dogma by looking at my life. (Think of me as your personal crash-test dummy of enlightenment.)

I think you would laugh if you saw me writing this book right now. I've got my headphones in. I'm blasting high energy trance dance music. I'm smiling. I'm shaking my booty. I'm wearing my ripped jeans. I've got my funky glasses on, and I'm so high on life I can barely keep from erupting into joyous giggles.

I don't follow rules. You won't find me wearing any robes. I love to meditate, but I meditate to crazy music that shouldn't be relaxing. I operate outside of social norms. I only follow protocol when it feels right to me. I'm unbound. Completely free.

You ready to join me?

Here's a story that just about sums up Recontextualization.

Two professional baseball umpires were getting trained by a master umpire.

Sitting in the dugout waiting to go on the field for training, the master umpire turned to the pair and asked, "How do you call a strike?" The younger novice was eager to jump in. With lots of animated enthusiasm, he squatted down like he was waiting for a pitch to come in and started giving his commentary. "I've got my eye on the pitcher. He winds up and throws it. Like a hawk, I keep my eye on the ball. I look to see where the ball comes in. If it's in the strike zone, I call it."

The master umpire raised one eyebrow, sat in silence, arms folded, and nodded to the more experienced of the pair. "What you do think?"

Having more confidence and poise, the second professional umpire was much more matter of fact, "If it's in the strike zone, then it's a strike!"

The master umpire looked down and shook his head in disappointment.

Both students looked at each other confused. They both felt like there could be no other answer. In their minds, it's either in the strike zone or it's not. You call it like you see it.

Finally, the master umpire broke his silence and looked up with a smile. "Boys, the ball ain't nothin' 'till you call it."

It Ain't Nothin' 'Til You Call It

What you see... what you experience... it's all a lie your mind is telling you. You have been tricked into believing that your life is what it is.

In other words, your life is what your mind tells you it is. And you have never been asked to confront it, question it, or bust it.

What you see and what you experience is just a likely story. Your mind's description of your life and the happenings of your life is just your mental approximation.

If I asked you to describe the environment you are in right now, you would do a dismal job. Your description would barely scratch the surface of the complexity, the beauty, the order, the chaos, the micro, the macro, the inter-connectivity, the relationships between things, and the functionality. You could use millions of words, and it would barely do it justice.

As a practicality, your mind approximates and abbreviates. It uses old references to describe new situations. It links unrelated things to make sense of what it is experiencing.

In the coming chapters, I will assist you in completely pulling apart the insanity and distortions of your mind so that you can experience the profound bliss and overwhelming perfection of the world you live in. For now, I'm going to say it to you very simply.

Your life ain't nothin' 'til you call it. Everything that is happening "to you" is just a story you are telling yourself to try and make sense of it.

Here's one of the key questions that will help you rise out of the suffering of the mind and start living in an enlightened state...

> *"If you are going to make up stories, why not make up stories that feel good and empower you?"*

That's the power of Recontextualization. It's the skill of describing the conditions and circumstances in a way that creates an empowering reality for you.

From an Enlightened Perspective, there is not one fixed reality. From an Enlightened Perspective, there is an infinite number of realities to choose from. Unfortunately, your mind is wired to see things one way and then move forward from there. This creates the feeling of being stuck. When you are stuck, you are frustrated, defensive, and agitated. In that state, you literally short circuit and your life stops flowing.

The great news for you is this: Life isn't one way. Life is only what you say it is. So you can say something else and become empowered.

> *Did you catch that? Life isn't one way. Life is only what you say it is. You can say something else and become empowered.*

When I make that statement my clients and students typically have the following reaction: "Okay, sure Matthew. I'm going to just bury my head in the sand and say pretty things and life is going to change. Come on!! What about reality? What about science? Isn't science defining the probable, measurable, tangible world?

Isn't science proving that our stories about reality aren't true and there is a factual, true, replicable, and concrete reality?"

Take a deep breath. Yes, of course, science is doing that. And thank God!! But science doesn't help you when your boss is being an unreasonable jackass, does it? NO!

Science has a job. Describe the physical reality of our experience in a factual, provable, replicable, and indisputable way.

Enlightenment has a different job. Describe the contextual experience of a human being's life in a way that brings profound joy, certainty, confidence, and a feeling of oneness with all that is.

If you are curious, I encourage you to find science that supports the intuitive insights of enlightened people. But, I'll let you find that on your own. This book isn't about that.

You may not know I'm a total science geek. I find it deeply meaningful. I also find that most people just want to discover the keys to living a happy life. Some science will help, but most doesn't matter. For example, you can find scientific proof that human beings influence machines with their consciousness. But knowing about that phenomenon isn't making anyone enlightened.

Normal or Enlightened, You Choose

Normal People: Your mind talks to you. You listen like it's the truth. You take action based on misinformation and illusions. Your life sucks more than it needs to.

Enlightened People: Your mind tells you a story. You acknowledge that it's just a story. You notice that it stems from a biological drive to survive. You realize it has nothing to do with reality. You consciously decide to create a new meaning. You take action based on your authentic desires. Your life kicks ass.

Normal people take their mind at face value and live a life with too much suffering, unfulfilled desires, and frustration.

Enlightened people see their mind as a biological mechanism that is designed to help them navigate the world. They recognize its limitations and use Recontextualization to stay deeply connected to their joy, no matter what life throws at them.

Context

Context is defined as the parts of speech that precede and follow a word or passage and contribute to its full meaning, as in, it is unfair to quote out of context.

In other words, the descriptors you use give the situation its meaning. The meaning you give a situation determines your reaction to it. Your reaction creates your reality. What is your goal? I assume it is joy, peace, power, grace, bliss (with a little prosperity mixed in for fun). The only thing standing in the way of your experiencing that enlightened state is your description of life.

Isn't it crazy? That's how much power you have. I know it's a little hard to believe right now.

Another definition of context is the conditions and circumstances that are relevant to an event.

Recontextualization is the skill of describing the conditions and circumstances in a way that creates an empowering reality for you. You create your experience with your words. You choose the descriptors, and therefore, you create your experience.

Oftentimes my students process that statement incorrectly.

When I say you create your experience, I don't mean you create reality. There is a broader reality in the world that is beyond you or your control. But no one controls your experience of that reality except you.

Here's an example. You have a big meeting scheduled. You wake up that morning and you think to yourself, "I'm tired. I want to stay in bed." Is that language empowering you? If you have to get up and go to work and be productive that day, then the answer is no.

"I'm tired, and I want to stay in bed," is most likely sort of resistance to either how things are, or how the mind (The Drunk Monkey) thinks things will be.

To transform the experience called "I'm tired" let's create a Recontextualization to see it from an Enlightened Perspective.

Remember, Recontextualization is just learning to talk about things differently.

You might say something like this...

"Yes, this feeling is what I call 'tired.' I admit that I have an unrealistic expectation that my body will be peppy, alert, and ready for a great day when I wake up. It's just a story I have about my body.

I'm not very realistic about this. My body is unpredictable in the morning. I estimate that I'm energized 1 out of 100 times in the morning.

Okay, let's be honest. I'm resisting the way my body wakes up. I'm resisting the feeling that I have right now.

I am pretending that I am the authority on my physiology, and I deem its current state inappropriate.

This is stupid. I'm not an authority on physiology. I just have some illogical expectation that it should be peppy in the morning.

If I'm being honest with myself, it takes some time for this body to get going. But it always gets going. I don't need to worry about it. Even when I have a restless night's sleep and I have to get up to meet an obligation, my body always rallies. I get the job done.

There is no rule that says I can't take a nap later if I need one.

Time to get up. You made a promise. This is your life. This is your meeting. You said yes. You made the plans. Your body isn't cooperating right now, but it will come around."

Recontextualization is the skill of describing the conditions and circumstances in a way that creates an empowering reality for you.

It starts with awareness. If you can't notice the mind telling you stories that are degrading your experience of life, then you will never enlighten.

Don't worry, at the back of the book **I'm going to give you 23 Daily Practices you can use** to make sure I fulfill my promise of teaching you to fulfill Quiet Mind Epic Life.

The Mind Believes Life is Fixed

It's arrogant to think that life is static and fixed as is. Right now, in this moment, you can step back and see the world from an Enlightened Perspective.

Close your eyes and just reflect on the never-ending progression of change that you have experienced in your life. Your relationships are not the same as they were 10 years ago. Your experience of work is not the same. You're different now. You are not the same person you once were. You are changing. Every aspect of your life mentally, emotionally, and spiritually is changing. Everything in your broader environment is changing.

The mind doesn't like that. Change is not safe. To make sense of the world, the mind assesses. It labels things. It puts every part of your life in neat and tidy boxes. It categorizes, "He's like that. She does it that way. Watch out for those things over there. I'm fat. My wife is negative, I'm not as smart as others. I need to try harder to get the same results" on and on it judges, defines and labels.

These labels become the filter through which you see life. You stop seeing things as brand new. You don't see the changes in people or situations because the mind has everything labeled and put into what it considers their proper place.

The mind is like an arrogant scientist walking around with one of those labeling machines. The mind never takes the time to verify things. The mind has no time for that. The mind is arrogant and, therefore, profoundly ignorant. It believes that its stories are true and that's that.

"I'm like this..."

"John's like that..."

"Airports are..."

"This city is a pain in the ass."

The mind labels on autopilot and then lives like the labels are what life is. In the meantime, everything keeps changing, shifting, and transforming.

Let's be honest. Most of the time the mind is completely out of date on what's happening and who people are.

The mind reflects, "I walked over and pet my neighbor's dog when I was ten, and it bit me. Therefore, all dogs bite."

Now you are in your current life. You see a dog, and your body is inconveniently filled with chemicals that put you in fight or flight mode. It takes the past and puts it in the future.

Your body reacts with a singular message, "YOU ARE IN DANGER!!"

Your mind lives in illusions and distortions of reality it creates for itself. One dog bit, but all dogs don't bite.

It's arrogant to think that your perspective is accurate. Life is too complex for the mind to comprehend. The mind has to simplify every one of your experiences to make sense of it.

Therefore, it misses almost everything because it's so busy trying to correlate the past to the present in order to predict the future.

When your mind goes completely quiet, and the pointless labeling and predicting stop, you get connected to the perfection of it all. The vastness and the infinite nature of existence are overwhelming. Have you ever seen a beautiful sunset and felt emotional? You ever watch an emotional movie and feel touched?

These become pervasive states when the mind is quiet.

Once you see that your mind is completely full of crap and doesn't know anything about anything, it will start to go quiet. You will then start to feel that overwhelming joy all the time. This happens because you are able to take in the complexity of life without having to put it into a category or box. You will just breathe in the beauty and the grandeur and be in awe at the amazing universe you are living in right now. When you are in a profound state of gratitude and awe, everything gets better.

Using Recontextualization, you will learn to change the meaning of the conditions and circumstances of your life, which changes your responses to those conditions. New actions can effortlessly move your life in the direction you desire.

As an enlightened person, you admit that your perspective on life is not accurate. It is just your perspective.

A normal person says, "This is how it is."

The enlightened person says, "This is how I see it."

A normal person says, "That guy's a jerk."

The enlightened person says, "I keep resisting the way that guy behaves and making myself feel bad in the process."

The enlightened person recognizes that there is an infinite number of realities you can choose.

If you are going to make things up, why not make things up that feel good?

Asking yourself this question is a Recontextualization that gives you power in the moment.

You have to ask yourself, "Why have I been so committed to describing my life in a way that creates limitations?" If you haven't noticed, people are breaking the rules all the time. So why are you so committed to following them? Why are you limiting yourself with untrue, unfounded mental reactions like, "I'm not like those people who have it all. You don't understand my situation."

The mental reaction I just described is motivated by an unconscious drive to survive called Illogical Rules. If you are going to enlighten and stay enlightened, then you must learn to spot these Illogical Rules and neutralize them.

Illogical Rules are one of 10 Hidden Motives to Survive. I take you on a deep dive through the Hidden Motives later in the book. But first, let's sum up the power of Recontextualization.

Change your perspective, and the situation will change

When the mind stops talking, you are no longer burdened by its illogical judgments, assessments, rules, and illusions.

That means you can begin to deliberately create perspectives that empower you.

Recontextualization is the skill of describing the conditions and circumstances in a way that creates an empowering reality for you.

Perspective determines how you feel. How you feel influences your actions. Your actions create your results. You must remove the motive for the mind to think.

And that's exactly what we are about to do.

Chapter 8
Piercing Through The Denial Mechanism: Muscle Testing

To achieve Quiet Mind Epic Life, you must go beyond the ideologies, the stories, and the programming of the mind.

Your consciousness is being influenced by Hidden Motives to Survive. Those motives create talking in your head. You and I call that talking, "The Drunk Monkey."

The Drunk Monkey is a reaction. It has a group of Unconscious Reflexes that dominate your consciousness and distract you from the truth of your existence. For example, Forecasting the Negative is an Unconscious Reflex that distracts you from experiencing the present moment.

Unconscious Reflexes are strategies The Drunk Monkey uses to protect, avoid, and fix what its deemed a problem or a threat.

All the while, you are complete and perfect exactly as you are, right now. Nothing needs changing or fixing. Nothing needs to be added or subtracted.

Unfortunately, that perspective is useless to The Drunk Monkey. On examination, you'll see The Drunk Monkey rejects that idea. It denies that a reality other than what it has invented is even possible.

The Drunk Monkey has a position on everything, including you and your place in the world. The Drunk Monkey has you convinced that its opinions about you are correct. That you are, in fact, broken and in need of fixing. That if you could just get better at this or that, then your life would be better. The Drunk Monkey is convinced that if you were better, then you would have a better chance at survival.

These are just arbitrary points of view that have been genetically and culturally encoded into our consciousness. They don't have any real concrete validity. And, for the most part, they create negative feelings.

The stories The Drunk Monkey tells you create limitations that aren't really there. The only tool The Drunk Monkey has in its toolbox are likely stories. Stories that keep you limited.

The Marathon and The Hurt Knee

Until I was 32 years old, I believed that I couldn't run. When I was a pre-teen I hurt my knee, and I was unable to do sports after that.

In my thirties, I was surging into my new awareness and realized that my limitations were just stories I told myself.

One of my best friends at the time challenged me. He suggested that if it's all just a story, then I should use the techniques I've developed to coach my clients. It was time to overcome my knee story and run a marathon.

The Drunk Monkey was quick to comment with its negative forecasting, "Don't do it. You could really hurt yourself!"

Using rudimentary versions of the techniques I use today, I challenged The Drunk Monkey. I designed an experiment that included running really short distances to test the hypothesis: If I run, I will hurt my bad knee.

With each new distance achieved, I scoffed at The Drunk Monkey and felt more and more power.

After six months, I ran a marathon! 26.2 miles complete. At the end of the race, I felt very proud of myself, so I decided to call my mom to tell her that I had finally overcome this life-long bad knee problem.

I told her the good news and of course, she was very proud of me for running a marathon, given I'd never been an athlete. But she was also very confused. Mom told me I never had a problem with my knee when I was a kid. She said I hated sports and would do anything to get out of having to participate in school.

You should have seen my face! I had been living my life as if my knee was permanently damaged and I could not run or play sports. **It turns out, that was just a story I had told myself when I was a kid to get out of having to participate, and my mind had adopted this story as the truth.**

It was so real for me that, up until age 32, I would categorically reject anything related to sports. "Oh, I'm sorry, I can't do that.

I've got a bad knee!" What the hell? That's The Drunk Monkey in action.

On investigation, you'll see that The Drunk Monkey uses a denial mechanism to keep you safe. It is convinced things are one way, and it denies that they could be another. The mere idea that it has incorrectly assessed a situation is a threat, so The Drunk Monkey collects more evidence to prove its position is valid.

This is how I spent my teens to my thirties believing I had a bad knee.

The Power of Admitting Your Life is a Lie

Okay, here's the bad news. It turns out that every single thing you believe about yourself, your life, the people in your life, and the circumstances of your life is exactly like my knee. Just a story. Not true. Not real. A flimsy story, that once challenged, will crumble like a sand castle in the wind.

> When you let go of the assumption that you know anything, that you know what has happened in your life, that you know what is happening right now, you release the lie that you know who you are, and that you know what life is and how it all works, then YOU ARE FINALLY FREE. It is the most em-powering, delicious experience of your life.

The Drunk Monkey fears that admitting your life is a story will put you in danger. The Drunk Monkey does its best to know everything about everything in order to steer you away from bad things and towards good things.

It fears the idea that your perception of reality is, at best, just a guess, and estimation. It wants to hold onto the belief that you know what and how the world is.

We can't fault The Drunk Monkey for that perspective. By creating agreement with others, labeling things and creating expectation, we have learned to function in this world. We have learned to survive.

And while we have done a tremendous job creating safer conditions that are very comfortable, we are still riddled with doubts, insecurities, and fears.

That's because the entire premise of The Drunk Monkey is flawed. The Drunk Monkey doesn't know anything about anything. It just has a label or a story or an expectation or a fantasy that it creates to help you survive in a world where you will eventually die.

When you finally admit that you don't know anything, when you finally release your motive to think, you are overwhelmed with joy.

All the loss The Drunk Monkey feared turns out to be the exact opposite. It's a major advantage to have a quiet mind, unburdened by the assumption that you know things. It is profound

QUIET MIND EPIC LIFE

to realize that you don't know what is actually happening, ever.

Instead, you become curious. Quiet mind creates the conditions for curiosity, seeking to understand. There is a pervasive feeling of awe and overwhelming feelings of love and certainty.

You have spent your life at the mercy of the stories The Drunk Monkey tells you. Those stories are the source of all your suffering. That's the impact of the mind. Now I want to introduce you to the stories your *body* tells you.

Your Body Tells A Different Story

As you know by now, I'm like you. I have been a seeker most of my life. I admit that at times I go a little overboard. My soul appears to have an insatiable thirst for understanding. It has driven me my whole life.

In 1999 my father had a mastermind group that I was a part of. He invited Wayne Dyer to speak to us and spark a deeper discussion on spirituality. At the meeting, he told us that there was one book we should read if we truly wanted to quantum leap in our understanding of the world. My heart skipped a beat. I thought, "You are speaking my language!"

The book was Power vs. Force by David R. Hawkins. I devoured it. In fact, it was the first book I ever read twice back to back. Inside Dr. Hawkins discussed a proven, but seemingly esoteric, discernment tool called Applied Kinesiology, more commonly known as Muscle Testing.

Applied Kinesiology is the process of testing the body's strength or weakness after exposure to stimuli. A simple example: I ask you to think about a time in your life when you felt bad. If the conditions are correct (which is tricky), I could push down on your outstretched arm and the muscle holding up your arm would go weak. In essence, the thought (stimuli) would cause the body to malfunction.

As I've told you over and over in this book, I realized that taking things at face value because a teacher told me turned out to be a mistake. That's why early on I learned to put things to the test. I learned to question. I began to validate ideas and concepts for myself. I stopped relying on the Guru's word. (I will ask the same of you.) As a result, I have used my own experience to validate the claims of the authors and teachers I've studied.

Adding muscle testing to my process was a game changer. I spent countless hours, every day, trying to master Applied Kinesiology. Like any new skill, it was fickle, frustrating, and bewildering. There were moments when the technique was inaccurate. I exposed someone to what is known to make people weak and they would be strong. Ugh! I went back to the drawing board over and over until I could reproduce what my teacher had taught me.

I was hell-bent on proving or disproving the premise of Applied Kinesiology: true statements make the arm go strong and false statement make the arm go weak.

After nearly two decades of experimentation and being exhilarated by the results, deflated when it didn't work, blowing my family's mind, being ridiculed by naysayers, thinking that I was crazy and learning to be completely neutral, I mastered it.

The result was better than I could have ever imagined. But it was not exactly what my mentor had promised. I could not discern truth from falsehood. But, I could tell you what caused the body to function or malfunction. I could discern what was strong vs.. what was weak. In the end, that nuance turned out to be profoundly important.

The information I have been able to discern using Applied Kinesiology was the ultimate accelerator for becoming enlightened. It is THE REASON I am able to write this book and substantiate the information I am sharing with you.

Let me bring you up to speed, and then I will share some of the life-changing perspectives Applied Kinesiology has provided me.

The Foundation of Applied Kinesiology

Let me start with a question: Using your rational mind, is hate destructive or constructive to life?

For example; If someone advised you to say the word **hate** over and over again every day, would it have an effect on you?

You bet it would! As a high-conscious person, you innately know that "hate" is not uplifting.

Given you are this far into this book, it is safe to say that you realize that your words have a powerful effect on your reality.

If you said, "I hate you" to your child on a regular basis, you know with certainty that your words would create a degrading psychological reaction in your child. And now you know that it would actually create an imbalance in their consciousness.

When hate is present in consciousness, it is degrading. It creates a cyclone of tormenting mind chatter, and it destroys your spirit.

On the other hand, the word "love" is intuitively constructive and uplifting. If you hear "I love you" on a regular basis, it strengthens you and creates a balanced mental framework.

You know that your words have tremendous power over your mindset. But what you might not realize is that your words have just as much power over your physiology.

If you said the word "hate" over and over again while lifting weights, it would negatively affect your strength. Conversely, love would positively affect your ability to lift the weight.

The words you use affect the body's integrity. When the body is exposed to different words, it is either strengthened or weakened.

If you consistently played music that mentioned killing, degrading other people, hurting, being oppressive, or being aggressive, then your body and mind would be compromised. They would cease to function in a way that strengthened you.

You and I could use Applied Kinesiology to demonstrate a weak response to music that used those kinds of words, ideas, and concepts.

Even though words don't have a physical form, with Applied Kinesiology, you can visually see that they have a dramatic effect on your physical body.

This is not a foreign concept for you. You already live in a world where the unseen affects the seen.

If you live next door to a nuclear reactor that has been compromised and is leaking radioactive material, then your physical body would be gradually weakened and health problems would likely arise.

You can't see the radiation, just like you can't see the thoughts. But that doesn't mean it's not affecting you. It affects you whether you see it or not. It affects you whether you believe in radiation or not.

Quiet Mind Science Update

Over 100 years ago, quantum physicists determined that physical matter doesn't really exist, that everything is just energy in different states of vibration.

Nobel Prize winning physicist Werner Heisenberg once stated, "Atoms or elementary particles themselves are not real; they form a world of potentialities or possibilities, rather than one of things or facts."

You and I naturally relate to our bodies like they are solid matter. Yet, an electron microscope shows us something completely different. Molecules are made of atoms which are potentialities and possibilities, not physical stuff like our mind concludes. These subatomic particles exist within a field. Using your quiet mind, you begin to sense and interact with that field.

After nearly two decades of working with Applied Kinesiology, I've come to realize that words, phrases, ideas, concepts, and thoughts affect the body at the level of the potentialities and possibilities.

My insight is that the stimuli affect us at the energetic level, not the material level. I have discerned that we are being affected at the level of subatomic particles.

My teachers postulated, and I concur, that when you are testing the strength and weakness of a muscle in response to stimuli, you are "testing" consciousness itself.

If you say the word hate and then you test the strength of your muscle, then you will notice it's not as strong. It's weakened by the presence of the concept or what the word hate represents in consciousness.

A Note About Learning To Muscle Test:

If you are curious about learning to test, then I invite you to start the process. As I've said above, learning any new skill is challenging. Applied Kinesiology is no exception. The possibility of getting false readings are very high in the beginning.

I had no idea what I was getting myself into when I first committed to mastering Applied Kinesiology.

Remember, I'm teaching you concepts that came out of 18+ years of trial and error. I spent years in delight that were followed by years of hopelessness and frustration with this technique.

It's important that you don't allow The Drunk Monkey to get arrogant. Don't indulge your ego and believe that you will be able to replicate my findings with no skill and no mastery.

If you want to learn Applied Kinesiology for yourself, you will need to be *very patient* and diligent.

I like to say to my students, "If you want to climb Mount Everest, you don't just wake up one day and say, 'Okay! Today is the day.'" There are literally thousands of decisions, skills, considerations, and preparations necessary to safely ascend to the peak and make it back home alive.

Mastery of Applied Kinesiology is like any other skill set. It takes tens of thousands of hours to master.

To get the best results from the insights discerned from Applied Kinesiology, I request that you suspend your disbelief the same way you would if you were reading the story about a man who builds rockets.

If you read a book on how to build rockets, you suspend disbelief because you don't have the knowledge to understand the process of building rockets.

If you were inspired to do so, you could certainly test his rocket-building ideas. But you would lack the thousands of hours of understanding necessary to create a rocket, which simply means you would likely fail many times before you achieve a successful flight.

Here's the point. Your failure would not prove that his ideas were inaccurate. Your failure would only prove that you don't have the same knowledge and skill.

Applied Kinesiology presents us with ideas and concepts that are mind-bending and earth-shattering. So in the spirit of getting the most out of this book, you recognize that there are things you just don't know about.

Applied Kinesiology can be summed up into one statement:

What you expose yourself to will either strengthen your body or weaken it.

Most people apply pressure to another person's outstretched arm to test the strength or weakness. With practice, you can learn to practice on your own body.

I've done hundreds of thousands of tests since 1999. The insights that I've received from these tests form the basis of my mind going completely quiet.

Enlightened States are Simply Greater Levels of Integrity

Integrity is defined as the state of being whole and complete; the whole thing is working well, undivided, integrated, intact, and uncorrupted.

Applied Kinesiology shows you what is strengthening to the body. In other words, it shows you what creates integrity. When you are strong things work. When you expose yourself to something that is strengthening, then your body system is fortified and operates more effectively.

The stronger you are, the more power you have. When you are strong you are more creative, empowered, and resourceful. Like I discussed at the beginning of this book, everything speeds up when you are feeling peace, joy, and flow.

Mind Chatter is a Lack of Integrity

Your mind talks to you and disturbs your peace for one reason and one reason only: Threat.

When you are weak, things don't work. Your body/mind system is lacking in integrity, it's not fortified. It's corrupted. That is a compromised state, and it causes your mind to do its job and make sure you are not harmed. When you are weak or your system malfunctions, the mind begins to analyze, assess, judge, and strategize in order to keep you safe.

To put it very, very simply: Mind chatter is a sign of weakness present in your body/mind system. Something is out of alignment and is disturbing your natural balance.

Through extensive use of Applied Kinesiology, I've come to understand that words, thoughts, ideas, and concepts can affect you just like toxic waste. You can't expose yourself to something toxic and then expect to function at your best.

Using Applied Kinesiology, you are able to physically distinguish which words, phrases, thoughts, ideas, and concepts are "toxic" and which are "healthy" to you, represented by strength or weakness.

Strength can be represented by the idea that it is constructive to the body/mind system. Weakness can be represented by the idea that it is destructive. You get the idea.

Your Opinion Doesn't Matter

Applied Kinesiology is impartial. When done correctly, your opinions don't affect the results. Luckily, the background field of radiation that creates the subatomic particles in your muscles doesn't care about what you believe.

It is fortified by certain ideas and degraded by others. It really is that simple. Therefore, your muscles will function and go strong or malfunction and go weak independently of what you believe is true or real.

In other words, your opinion doesn't matter to your muscles. They operate independently of The Drunk Monkey and your survival system.

Thoughts, words, ideas, and concepts will disrupt the body and cause your muscle to malfunction. For example, your arm will go weak even if you believe the opposite of what is being presented.

This is great news.

Applied Kinesiology operates beyond dogma, ego, your opinion, your culture, and your faith. Your muscle will go weak or strong no matter how strongly you believe something to be true or false.

Your opinion CAN influence the test. But not because your opinion is valid. Your opinion is a word, thought, idea, or concept, and it has the same power to cause your body to malfunction.

When I expose your muscle to a concept that fundamentally contradicts everything you have ever been taught to believe, your body will literally shut down. The testing will no longer give you accurate results. You will receive false positives and false negatives.

It's taken me nearly two decades to learn how to spot these malfunctions, correct them, and get the body back into a place where testing works accurately.

The possibility of you getting false positives/negatives as a beginner is absolutely certain. There is a 100% chance that your testing won't work effectively at first. Just like there is a 100% chance you aren't going to fly a rocket the first time you try to build one.

With dedication, you can get there. It will take a willingness to question everything and test everything you question.

The insights I provide in this book do not require you to learn to muscle test. I'm simply providing the mental framework necessary for you to be positively affected by the insights without having to test on your own body.

For now, here's what you need to know. Confronting your beliefs may cause the body to go into a fight or flight mode. Testing does not work when the body is in fight or flight mode.

When the body is in fight or flight mode, you will start getting false positives. You can tell if the body is ready for muscle testing by testing four points on the body and one phrase. If you ever get a chance to see me test in-person, you will see me constantly testing these points on the body to make sure the testing is accurate.

Some foods or substances will read differently on different people. For example, sugar may go strong on one person and weak on another. Though there are certain substances that go weak on everyone.

Words, phrases, thoughts, ideas, concepts, images, and situations all read the same on everyone as long as they are ready for muscle testing and not in a fight or flight state.

Strong and Weak. Not True and Not False.

It's taken me years to deconstruct my natural instinct to arbitrarily relate to strong tests as true and weak tests as false.

I'm going to coach you see this nuance over and over. I do that because Applied Kinesiology is just strong and weak. Constructive and destructive. Nothing more. Nothing less. Not true. Not false.

I will say this over and over because the Recontextualization based tests that make up the Rapid Enlightenment Process are unbelievably confronting to most people.

While it's not my intention, the statements that I'm going to expose you to will have a two-stage effect. At first, The Drunk Monkey is going to start jumping up and down screaming its opinions about right, wrong, good, and bad. That's stage one. Then, suddenly and unexpectedly, the mind will start to go quiet. That's stage two.

That's the outcome we are looking for, right?

When The Drunk Monkey is going crazy, I am going to remind you over and over. What The Drunk Monkey thinks is not true! The statement just goes strong on the body, which simply means it is a strengthening idea. It creates integrity.

When I tell you statements that go weak, The Drunk Monkey will say, "Then it must not be true!" Nope! It just means they are statements that weaken the body. If you have a weakening statement stuck in your belief system, then your body will malfunction, your system will be imbalanced, and the body will have to compensate. One of those compensations is activation of The Drunk Monkey. The mind chatter will steal your peace.

Applied Kinesiology is Not a Crystal Ball

Finally, Applied Kinesiology is not predictive. It doesn't tell you the future. It tells you what is strong and what is weak on your body (or the body of the person doing the testing) now.

If you test a statement about the future, it will go strong or weak. But it won't tell you what is going to happen. It will demonstrate which words, phrases, thoughts, ideas, and concepts strengthen or weaken your body.

Why These Recontextualization Statements Quiet Your Mind

The Drunk Monkey is the mouthpiece of your survival system. It talks as a way of pushing or maneuvering the body away from harm and towards positive survival objectives.

When The Drunk Monkey experiences threat, it is triggered into action.

When you are thinking, speaking, or exposing yourself to ideas and concepts that weaken your system, you become imbalanced.

We have already discussed that the Hidden Motives are actually imbalances in consciousness. When you are exposed to any of the Hidden Motives, your arm will go weak when tested.

When you go through the healing processes I provide for each Hidden Motive, you start to remove that information from your system and it makes you stronger. This means that you become more aware of what isn't working for you. That makes you flexible. This additional flexibility provides you with new insights in the form of options. Those options give you new levels of personal power.

> Here's the bottom line. The statements I'm going to expose you to in the next section create an empowering context. As I've said, none of the statements are true. They are statements that universally go strong or go universally weak.

I am presenting these statements to you because, after thousands of tests, I've concluded that they will begin a progression towards an inevitable silencing of The Drunk Monkey.

These statements are just a context. The objective is to Recontextualize your fundamental beliefs about who you are and your existence. This is the path to a quiet mind.

Remember that context is not true or false. It simply contains the power to guide and direct your perspective and thus your behavior.

> A *new perspective creates new reactions. If you react differently, you will behave differently. New behaviors create new results.*

Recontextualization is the skill of describing the conditions and circumstances in a way that creates an empowering reality for you.

As you adopt the strong statements and reject the weak statements, you will become progressively more empowered.

I state again, "Not because they are true. Because they make you go strong."

Chapter 9
Quiet Mind Epic Life Recontextualization Statements

In Chapter 4 you discovered The Rapid Enlightenment Process helps you to achieve enlightened prosperity.

The process creates a state of everlasting peace where worry and fear become irrelevant. You rise above cultural conditioning, limiting dogma and unexamined beliefs.

In this free state, the of positions of the ego are abandoned.

Suddenly, all is forgiven. You see that all is well in the world. There is nothing to resist or push against.

In an enlightened state, suffering is transcended. As you realize nothing needs to be changed, altered or avoided.

The world is whole and complete exactly as it is. Urgency is replaced by a connection to your infinite nature.

As a result, accomplishment becomes effortless. Peace of mind is pervasive.

You are here on earth. You are participating in society. You might as well enjoy it.

The only thing standing between you and experiencing enlightened prosperity is dogma.

Your unexamined dogma creates a paradigm that is limiting your happiness, your success, and your self-expression.

There is no way to prove if your beliefs about yourself and the world are true. But... You still believe them. You defend your positions, points of view and perspectives like they are important for the well-being of the species. Sometimes you even act like your life depends on them.

In a nutshell, you are following rules that don't exist.

You are living via beliefs that limit you.

You defend perspectives that are a figment of your imagination.

You diminish yourself because you don't meet arbitrary standards

You are feeling bad because you don't measure up.

Cultural conditioning, dogma and limiting beliefs are tethers holding you back from ascending into enlightened states. They literally block you from the recognition that the source of life within you is the source of life in everyone and everything else. We are all one thing expressing itself with infinite variety.

The Rapid Enlightenment Process is a series of contextual shifts that destroy cultural conditioning, dogma and limiting beliefs and replaces them with new enlightened dogma.

As I like to say "if you are going to make things up, why not make things up that feel good?"

The Rapid Enlightenment Process recontextualizes the fundamental questions about the meaning of life, and your role in it, while striving to create the most empowering context possible.

Meaning, the Rapid Enlightenment Process exposes you to a new set of contexts that naturally cause you to move away from survival-based dogma and into enlightened dogma.

Below you will find a series of statements, that when exposed to them, begin to quiet the mind. They begin to diffuse The Drunk Monkey's need to protect you from danger with its constant barrage of needless assessing, judging, and trying to predict the future.

In a nutshell, these statements get The Drunk Monkey to shut up!

Alright, here we go. Buckle your seat belt. Some of these statements will seem perfectly reasonable, and others will be profoundly confronting.

1. *Every human being interested in creating a quiet mind has incarnated as a human being many times. Tests Strong.*

   Okay, I'm sorry for coming right out and smacking your Drunk Monkey in the face. If you were raised in Western Christian based faith like I was, this can be a rather jarring concept. Stick with me. I've got your back.

Let's start with this idea: *Every human being interested in creating a quiet mind has incarnated as a human being many times.* This is not a true statement. This is a statement that goes strong on every person I've tested it on.

As long as their body hasn't gone into a self-protective fight or flight state, this test goes strong on everyone.

If you and I worked together to create the proper conditions, it would go strong on you too. You would put your arm out. I would ask you to resist and not let me push it down. I would make the statement and then push down on your arm. Your arm would start to wobble, maybe tremble, and then start to fall to your side.

The concept that you have lived multiple human lifetimes is not true. At least there is no way at this moment for us to prove it.

This is very important. Take this next thought into your consciousness.

Your opinion on this subject is based on the people you were raised by. Reincarnation is not knowable. Yet, The Drunk Monkey will fight to keep its model of the world intact and dismiss this process without any evidence to the contrary.

The Drunk Monkey is a cynic. The Drunk Monkey makes up stories and defends them without the burden of proof.

The only thing I'm doing right now is telling you about what I can prove goes strong on your arm.

There is no truth to what I'm telling you.

So why is it so important to tell you these potentially damning things?

After I got over the initial shock at the outcome of this muscle test, I did tests on as many people as I could get my hands on. I pondered, meditated, and used Applied Kinesiology to understand why this was even relevant.

Here's my conclusion:

What you experience is a function of context; How you see the world. What you believe in general and about yourself, others, and the circumstances you find yourself in, determine your experience.

Two people can have the exact same thing happen to them, and yet, they have completely different experiences. Experience is dependent on context.

Let's just get really honest with each other here. Eyeball to eyeball. mano-a-mano. The fear of death is the driving force behind The Drunk Monkey and all the disturbances in your mind. You may not notice it. It runs in the background of your consciousness like the system software on your phone.

Fear of death drives the majority of your decisions. Even if you don't think it does.

To create Quiet Mind Epic Life, you must align with a context that recontextualizes the fears that plague all humans.

Death is the number one concern of all human beings even if they say it isn't.

Here's a question for you. What happens to your courage, your creativity, and your curiosity when you begin to live like this life is just one of many, and death is not an ending?

Remember my knee? I believed that my knee was not functioning, and it limited my physical activity.

If a person believes they are dumb because everyone told them they were dumb, then they will be limited by the context that creates, not the reality of their situation.

When your ancestors thought that the world was flat, they stayed close to shore. It was the context, not the reality that influenced their behavior.

The statements I am presenting in this chapter are Recontextualizations that are backed up by Applied Kinesiology. Which simply means they cause the muscle to go strong or weak. Nothing more.

The takeaway is very simple: Start relating to your life like you have reincarnated over and over again. Throw out your old story about death, and adopt a new one. Not because it's true...because it's empowering.

2. **Every human being interested in creating a quiet mind has incarnated as a human being on Earth more than once. Tests strong.**

I do this test to clarify and confirm the prior test.

3. **Every human being interested in creating a quiet mind has incarnated as a human being on Earth more than twice. Tests Strong.**

I do this test to verify.

4. **Every human being interested in creating a quiet mind has incarnated as a human being on Earth thousands of times. Tests Strong.**

Now, here we have four tests which all go strong, and seemingly contradict what fellow Christians and I were taught in Sunday School. If you are a Hindu or Buddhist, this is nothing new to you. For the Judeo-Christian types, this can be a very confronting.

But here's the important thing to note. These tests go strong on the body. They embody a context that is fortifying to your physical form. They create integrity.

As you embrace the context of these statements, you begin to unravel The Drunk Monkey's programs and conditioning.

What you believe about birth and death are not true. They are just stories passed down by other human beings.

You have no conclusive data about what happens after death. We also can't understand where we come from, other than biology, which many scientists seem to agree isn't the entire story.

It is conclusive that we die. The body is dead. We don't know what happens AFTER the body stops working. Many religions and cultures are "sure" they know what happens next.

It's all conjecture. That's where Applied Kinesiology can give us a different perspective. With muscle testing, we discern that the concept of "multiple human lifetimes" goes strong. I don't pretend to know what that means. What I know with certainty is that the context itself causes the mind to quiet.

Over the past decade, I have seen conclusively that people who adopt this perspective have a sharp reduction in fear. Less fear means less mind chatter. Less mind chatter means more courage, clarity, creativity, and resourcefulness. That's the recipe for Quiet Mind Epic Life.

Let's test the opposite and see what happens.

5. **Every human being interested in creating a quiet mind has only incarnated as a human being one time. Tests Weak.**

6. **People only have one human lifetime, and that's the end of their existence. Tests Weak.**

It's not false. It's weak. It is degrading to your body to think that you are only a human being one time, and then it's the end of your existence.

When you operate from that context, your muscles malfunction, and they aren't able to maintain strength.

The perspective that you only live one human lifetime and that's the end of your existence is just a made-up story.

You can choose that story if you would like. I've noticed that people who choose that context fall into states of apathy. They start to think, "Why bother? It's all pointless."

Or worse, anxiety drives you to get everything done. To do as much as possible before it's all over. While that seems like good "motivation," it is driven by fear. Fear robs you of Quiet Mind. So you accomplish a lot, but you have no peace or satisfaction as a result.

Let's look at some strong tests that create Quiet Mind Epic Life.

7. **Human beings choose to come to Earth. Tests Strong.**

   Don't let The Drunk Monkey fool you into argument and positionality on this one. This is not me trying to be right or convince you of anything. You don't know if we choose or not. Neither do I.

   I'm simply reporting to you what goes strong and weak on people's arms when I expose them to these statements.

   It is strengthening to your body to adopt the context that you chose to come to Earth.

   Let's test the opposite.

8. **Being born as a human being on Earth is completely random. Tests Weak.**

   The arm goes weak when you say this statement. That doesn't mean it's false. No one on Earth knows if this is true or not. Not a single person. But that's none of our concern. Our objective is to create a strong body and mind that is unburdened by fears and doubts.

When you choose the context that your birth was a choice *you* made, you are empowered. Nothing seems very serious. You lighten up.

Takeaway:

By adopting the context that you choose to be born as a human being, you can rise above the Hidden Motives To Survive called Victim. Suddenly you see that you are not a victim. You chose to be here.

9. **Human beings choose their geographic location on Earth before they are born. Tests Strong.**

10. **Human beings choose their parents before they are born. Tests Strong.**

11. **Every human being interested in creating a quiet mind has incarnated as a human being on Earth many times with their current parents, friends, and family members. Tests Strong.**

Remember: Not True! Strong! Are you getting this? The body is telling you something very important. It is telling you that, if you want to function with strength, then you should simply create the context that the people around you are all longtime comrades in your soul's journey.

It is strengthening to your body. It causes your body to function when you think these thoughts.

Takeaway:

What if you started to look at each of the people in your life as someone who you have incarnated with over many lifetimes? What happens when you relate to everyone like, "We all chose to come here and have this experience together"?

Let's look at the opposite.

12. **Human Beings do not choose anything regarding their birth. Tests Weak.**

13. **A human being's existence is coincidental. Tests Weak.**

14. **A human being's birth is completely random. Tests Weak.**

These tests demonstrate that the body is weakened by the concept that you are living a random life.

15. **The human body is an expression of what is traditionally called the soul. Tests Strong.**

By now you have to ask yourself, "If you've lived multiple human lifetimes, what exactly is doing the living?" It turns out that "you are a soul" tests strong.

16. **The soul is infinite. Tests Strong.**

Google dictionary defines infinite as "limitless or endless in space, extent, or size; impossible to measure or calculate". It tests strong that you are a soul and the soul that you are, is infinite. Limitless.

This drove test me to investigate thousands of thoughts, ideas, and concepts over the years.

Here is a grouping of statements that not only surprised me, but they mentally and emotionally freed me in ways that I could never fully express.

As you adopt these next statements, you literally sign The Drunk Monkey's death warrant.

17. **A human being born on Earth is similar to the soul taking a vacation. Tests Strong.**

Did you notice the words "similar to"? If you remove those two words, this statement goes weak. Meaning, I don't know the exact nature, nor have I been able to discern the exact nature of the soul being here on earth.

All I can tell you is that this statement goes strong on every single person I've ever tested it on, and there have been hundreds of people over the years.

Let's be honest. You can't know if it is true. I can't know if it is true. What you currently believe is not true or false. What I believe is not true or false. It's just a likely story.

What's worse is that I suspect that what you currently believe isn't nearly as empowering.

The idea that a human being born on Earth is similar to the soul taking a vacation is a breakthrough perspective. When I began to adopt this perspective, everything in my life became more enjoyable. Almost immediately I was more brave, bold, and audacious.

If I was on vacation, why not make the most of it? More fun. More adventure. More experiences. Less worry. Less stress.

Takeaway:

Think about this question: What if your life was just a vacation for your soul?

What if all the drama was your soul's holiday?

What if all the disasters, the negatives and everything else you have experienced was a holiday from being infinite?

We are just making things up here! We don't really know. We can't know. I'm simply using a strong test to extrapolate and create an empowering context.

It goes strong that you chose to come to Earth. It tests strong that you chose to come to Earth with the people you are currently on the planet with.

Let's dig deeper. You can imagine what happened when I stumbled on this line of thinking? When your mind is silent, these tests overwhelm you with joy and peace.

18. A soul incarnates on Earth in a human body to learn lessons. Tests Weak!

Weak! What? One of the most common new age thoughts of all time goes weak!

"Life is a vacation" goes strong! Are you getting this?

Again, this is not true or false - it is strong and weak. It weakens your body to use the context that your soul is here on Earth to learn lessons.

Honestly, this test threw me for a loop. Up until this time, I was a product of my mentors, teachers, and guides. I believed what they told me. I could regurgitate the standard gobbly goop about learning lessons with the power of a preacher telling stories of fire and brimstone.

Here's the natural question, "If we aren't here to learn lessons, then what is life all about?"

19. **A soul incarnates as a human on Earth to have an experience. Tests Strong!**

Experience?!? That's it? Just an experience? What about meaning? What about truth? What about justice? What about transforming the planet into a utopian Shangri La?

The ideas that we are here to learn lessons, find the truth, seek justice and transforming the planet all go weak. The only thing that tests strong is you are here to have an experience.

What's the purpose?

20. **The purpose of a soul incarnating on Earth as a human being is to experience. Tests Strong!**

I've tested hundreds of purposes and none of them test strong on anyone. The only thing that ever tests strong is "to experience."

That blew my mind. Which is the point. My mind went completely silent with the realization that death, hatred, negativity, murder, genocide, and every other negative experience I ever looked down upon was, in fact, as valid of an experience as any other!

Oh my God! This context is so liberating!

21. **Negative experiences are just as valuable to the soul as positive experiences. Tests Strong!**

   I've lived my life in The Personal Development Prison. In fact, I spent a huge part of my life hell-bent on removing negativity.

   It turns out, the joke was on me. Negativity is just as valuable to my soul as positivity. As soon as I embraced negativity as a valuable experience on my soul's vacation, negativity virtually disappeared.

   Can you see how this context is causing your mind to quiet down?

   Remember this entire thing is completely invented. All I'm telling you is what went strong or weak. It tests strong that negative and positive experiences are equally valuable to your soul.

   So let's do what humans do. Let's extrapolate and make up stories based on this new context which is what I call Recontextualization.

   Think about it like this. If:

   • a soul chooses to come to Earth...

- a soul chooses its geographic location and parents...

- incarnating on Earth in your body is similar to taking a vacation for your soul...

- the soul's purpose for incarnating is to experience...

- negative experiences are as valuable to a soul as positive experiences...

Then, do you really need to save a child born with AIDS in Africa?

If the tests above are an empowering context to your body, then we can extrapolate that the African child chose that experience.

Most of my students start saying, "Mayday Mayday Mayday!!! You've gone too far, Matthew!!"

Stick with me here.

I'm not saying don't help. I'm asking you to align with what makes you strong. That child is a soul. That soul is infinite. That soul chose to come to Earth for a vacation. That soul chose its geography and its parents who happen to be infected with AIDS.

If we are extrapolating, then it stands to reason that the soul of that child thought this would make an interesting vacation filled with interesting experiences. If you are infinite, then none of it is actually negative.

Now, don't take this the wrong way. If you are inspired to help, then have at it. Go help!

But, if you are helping out of some delusion that you are saving the planet and making it a better place, then you are reacting to a set of ideas that test weak. No one asked for your help. You are not obligated to right ever wrong declared by The Drunk Monkey.

This is a book is about Quiet Mind Epic Life. I am committing to delivering to you a series of contexts that go strong with muscle testing, and cause the mind to go quiet.

If you are empowered by helping where you feel compelled to help, if it brings you profound peace, then help! If it makes you upset and angry at the world and makes your mind go crazy, then you may want to consider doing something else. Meaning, if you are helping because it is "needed" then you are responding to a position created by the mind. When you align with statements that go strong, and you see the helping is an experience you want to have, then you are free to choose.

I personally get incredible satisfaction out of helping other people. But only when they ask. That's how I am doing my vacation. You get to have your own vacation. My opinion doesn't count.

22. **The world needs to be saved. Tests Weak.**

23. **The world needs to be fixed. Tests Weak.**

24. **People are broken. Tests Weak.**

25. **People need to be healed. Tests Weak.**

It turns out that most of the old, pedestrian new age thinking tests weak. Which was initially sad for me. I used to get so much juice out of playing the role of a member of the spiritually elite who was here to bless the planet with my "specialness".

It took work to get over the idea that I wasn't special and that my purpose wasn't to save the other humans on the planets from themselves with my superior view on things. It only tests strong that I'm here to have an experience. The more I've embraced that context, the more peace I've felt.

Everyone is whole, complete, and perfect exactly as they are, from the most demonic to the most angelic. In fact, demonic/angelic labels are just delineations of the mind.

Mass murderers are just as important and valuable as the great saints.

They all came for a vacation.

There is nothing to fix. Nothing to correct. No one to blame, admonish or point the finger at.

Okay. Let's make a transition into some more mind-bending tests that came to me over the years and completely revolutionized my perspective on life.

26. **Each soul chooses how it will die as a human and the time of its human death before incarnating as another human being. Tests Strong!**

Wait? What? I just about fell over when this idea came to me. We choose our death before we come to Earth. Why? What is the benefit of that? What about free will?

27. **How you die and when you die is unknowable in human form. Tests Strong!**

Okay, now I'm confused. Why do we choose before we come, and then we can't know while we are here?

28. **A human being's death is completely random. Tests Weak!**

I had to test it just to make sure. It tests weak on every person I've tested on.

29. **A human being's death is similar to the soul giving the remaining humans the gift of an experience. Tests Strong!**

This is radical, I know. There is no benefit in me telling you this if it doesn't test strong on everyone. But it does. Death is a gift to the people you leave behind.

The sadness. The regret. The time of self-reflection. The pondering of our own looming death. These are all gifts that our family and friends give to us.

I remember not being able to comprehend why my cousins died in a car accident before they were even 10 years old. It was a devastating blow to my aunt and the whole family.

Yet, looking at it through this new lens, I can see how it galvanized the family. After my aunt's grief subsided there was a renewed energy for life. Powerful gifts!

30. **The soul arranges a select few negative experiences before incarnating as a human being on Earth. Tests Strong!**

This was very difficult to comprehend. Yet it tests strong. I have spent countless hours pondering and meditating on this context.

I extrapolate that we put some big rocks in our path to create new experiences. If you and I were muscle testing together, we could go through the really big negative experiences of your life and confirm that your soul arranged those negative experiences with others as a way of creating experiences.

Isn't that crazy? If you are like me, you have spent your entire life trying to avoid negative experiences. I've had such a drive to be positive, upbeat and happy. With Applied Kinesiology it tests strong that I intentionally arranged the big negative experiences of my life before I came to Earth. Wow.

This completely changed my relationship to negative experiences. Now I just experience them. The same way I experience riding a roller coaster. My body fills with adrenaline, The Drunk Monkey starts going crazy, and I just take it all in.

In situations where I might have felt anger or hostility in the past, I find myself saying, "Nice experience!" Sometimes I chuckle, and in my mind, I thank the other person for providing me with such a negative thing.

It's still negative. I still have the bodily reactions. The only difference is my mindset. I witness it. I feel bad. The negativity is real. And I'm *noticing* it rather than *being* it.

Apparently, that's the experience I am having this time around! I suspect the same for you.

I mean, come on. Can we just be honest here? If you are still reading this crazy book, then you and I are clearly connected. This ain't our first rodeo together. Hopefully, we will get a chance to look each other in the eye and say, "Hi Friend! Good to see you again."

Are you feeling it? Your mind is doing exactly what I said. At first, it fights it. Then it starts to malfunction like a computer freezing up. Eventually. it's going to reboot and the mind is going to be much more quiet. Yeah! High Five!

Okay, let's keep going. I have so much more to tell you. These last 10 years have been indescribably empowering and enlightening. Ready for more?

So many of my friends say, "Matthew? What about free will?" Let's test.

31. **A soul has free will while it is incarnated as a human being. Tests Strong!**

And yet, it tests strong that the soul arranges a select few negative experiences as a way of stirring things up and making life interesting. Based on my experience, there does not seem to be a set number of negatives. Everyone is different.

The negative experiences provide new probabilities based on the conditions that are present. In the moment you get to choose. Obviously, you are choosing through all the other clutter and information contained within your consciousness which creates even more potentiality.

32. The life experiences of a human being are completely random. Tests Weak.

33. Every human experience is predestined. Tests Weak!

It weakens your body to live from the context that your life experiences are completely random. Conversely, it also weakens the body to believe that your life is predestined.

34. The soul arranges negative human experiences to create new experiential probabilities. Tests Strong.

You choose the negative experiences as a way of spicing things up. You want to create some new experiences. We can extrapolate that you get together with your other soul buddies and make plans to negatively impact each other.

So next time something really bad happens to you, you now have the opportunity to say, "Hmm? Nice choice of experiences. This really sucks! I don't like this at all!" and that can lead you to say, "I wonder what new experience will come from this? What should I create? What can I do with this?" Bam! Suddenly you are the witness rather than the victim.

Let me remind you again: This is not true. This tests strong on the body. These concepts are not currently knowable via a scientific method. They may never be.

Everything that you and I believe about life and death was what we were told. It's all myth. It's all conjecture. Your guess is about as good as mine. I'm simply sharing what goes strong and weak using Applied Kinesiology.

35. **The vast majority of souls that incarnate as a human on Earth have a dominant desire for negative experiences. Tests Strong.**

What the heck!?! The majority of people "want" negative experiences? That didn't seem possible to me. I have spent my entire life believing that people are moving towards positive experiences.

It turns out that my "everyone wants to be positive" context tests weak. The only thing that tests strong is that the majority of souls incarnate to intentionally have negative experiences.

Now you have to admit that sounds crazy. But let's do some extrapolating. It's only negative because we call it that. Look around your life. What is the ratio of positive people to negative people? Pretty heavily weighted towards negative most likely.

Apparently, that is a very popular vacation for a soul. Apparently having a positive experience on Earth is not very popular at all. No wonder most people think you and I are weird.

Most people actually believe that happy people are just stupid people who don't understand what's actually happening in the world.

Sorry. You and I are the weirdos. The majority of the people are here to enjoy a holiday filled with negativity.

What if you just started smiling when you saw your friends and family having negative experiences? What if you started to think, "Nice vacation! I love all the drama and hate you are creating."

Can you see how this perspective literally melts away your resistance and negativity?

When you align with statements that cause your body to go strong, you align with thriving based consciousness. The Drunk Monkey's job becomes irrelevant, and you naturally move away from surviving based contexts to thriving contexts.

As a result, you begin to transcend the mind altogether.

The Rapid Enlightenment Process is a series of contextual shifts that destroy limiting dogma and replace it with new dogma that causes you to spontaneously enlighten.

By now, I suspect your mind is simultaneously racing and more at peace. You are taking in and processing these muscle tests, and replacing existing dogma with new enlightened dogma.

There are four components of The Rapid Enlightenment Process

1. Seeing the mind as a survival mechanism: The Drunk Monkey. (*Chapter 5*)

2. Understanding what causes The Drunk Monkey to talk: The Hidden Motives To Survive. (*Chapter 6*)

3. Transcending the mind's limiting dogma: Recontextualization. (*Chapter 7*)

4. Piercing through the veil of the denial mechanism: Muscle testing. (*Chapter 8*)

You've just completed the Quiet Mind Epic Life Recontextualizations. Congratulations. These are Enlightened Perspectives that cause your mind to go quiet.

Now, we go even deeper.

In the following chapters, you will begin developing the skill to neutralize the Unconsciousness Reflexes of The Drunk Monkey. Awareness of these Unconscious Reflexes gives you a huge advantage in life. When you witness your survival based biology firing off, you can deliberately shift your perspective along with the resulting actions you take. You literally go from being unconscious to being conscious in the moment.

Once you see how The Drunk Monkey uses the Unconscious Reflexes as strategies for keeping you safe, we will dive into the underlying cause; The Hidden Motives To Survive.

As you see the link between The Hidden Motives To Survive and the Unconscious Reflexes of The Drunk Monkey, you have the power to release the limiting dogma they create and replace it with enlightened dogma.

The result: your mind quiets and you are free to create your version of an epic life, unburdened.

Next, let's explore The Drunk Monkey's Unconscious Reflexes.

Here we go.

Chapter 10
The Unconscious Reflexes of The Drunk Monkey

The doctor taps your knee with his hammer. Your leg twitches. It's a reflex. You can't help it. You look into the rearview mirror of your car, and there are police lights flashing. Your heart rate increases. It's a reflex. Some people see blood, and they instantly feel sick. It's a reflex.

To get you to comply with its biological motives, The Drunk Monkey uses what I call Unconscious Reflexes.

Unconscious is defined as the part of the mind that is inaccessible to the conscious mind but can affect behavior and emotions.

Reflex is defined as an action that is performed as a response to a stimulus and without conscious thought.

The recognition of Unconscious Reflexes is the result of decades of studying the survival mind.

Creativity, love, joy, optimism, happiness, compassion, acceptance... these thoughts do not live in the realm of The Drunk Monkey. They are not possible when you are in a survival state.

It is vital you see this dynamic as we explore the Unconscious Reflexes of The Drunk Monkey and the Hidden Motives To Survive that trigger them.

Of course, we are not going to tiptoe into this lightly. Instead, we are going to start by taking on one of the most prevalent and impactful Unconscious Reflexes of them all: Forecasting The Negative.

Chapter 11
Forecasting The Negative

Forecasting The Negative is one Unconscious Reflex that The Drunk Monkey uses to try and avoid negative consequences by forecasting what potential negatives might happen in the future.

• •

The Drunk Monkey accidentally thinks it is psychic and can predict the future. It invents a future, pretends it is real, and then behaves accordingly.

• •

In other words, The Drunk Monkey pretends that it is psychic and can tell the future in an effort to avoid pain and gain pleasure.

If we are being honest, that is a pretty awesome survival system. I mean, come on! When your ancestors were walking through the plains and suddenly there was a rustling sound in the bushes, this ability to estimate enabled them to avoid being ambushed by an oncoming predator!

Forecasting negative futures is really, really useful when you are actually in dangerous situations. You want this functionality when you are trying to cross a busy street. If you are out hiking, then forecasting the negative is very useful.

But, for most of life, it is not useful at all. Unfortunately, for you and I, these Unconscious Reflexes are hard-wired into our thinking. We get bombarded with unwanted negative information when we are trying to do something awesome with our life.

Here's an example from my own life.

I estimate my mind is quiet around 90%+ of the time. But, enlightened or not, I'm still human. Becoming enlightened takes intentional focus. Staying enlightened takes just as much intentional focus.

That said, I'm still an animal with biological drives. I'm a normal person: married, two ex-wives, four kids, debts, assets, three businesses, cash flow to manage, hobbies, aspirations, limitations, and other considerations.

That is to say, I am confronted with Unconscious Reflexes, just like you.

"Hi. My name is Matthew Ferry. I'm a human being."

I'm just a human being who was driven to achieve Quiet Mind Epic Life. Fifty years of life and I have the tools to rise above the negativity and experience enlightened states. But I still get up every morning, sometimes tired, and as they say, "Fight the good fight." My biology still sneaks in there and tries to keep me safe.

To drive this point home, let's examine a recent Forecasting The Negative experience I had.

Here's the back channel. I'd spent the better part of a decade trying to escape my reputation for being a great sales trainer. When I left that world years ago, I was really good at it, and thousands of people were disappointed that I wasn't offering the programs I was known for.

At that time, I was committed to becoming known as a mindset coach. I realized that sales and business blocks were mental, and I had developed some powerful solutions to combat them.

For the better part of a decade, I worked almost exclusively in the real estate industry and on Wall Street. I helped brass tacks business people be more productive using mindset strategies.

But suddenly, I had this inspiration to go all the way as a mindset coach. I had been teaching the dynamics of The Drunk Monkey for 24 years by then. First as a part of my sales training and now more broadly in my mindset methodology. In the process, I had entered an enlightened state.

I became fascinated with helping others achieve this state shortly after it happened to me. I have been teaching various iterations of The Rapid Enlightenment Process to my private clients and my private mastermind for about a decade. I even hosted an event called, "Breakthrough to Bliss" for a few years working with small groups and perfect this system.

But I never declared myself a spiritual teacher.

Here comes The Unconscious Reflex called Forecasting The Negative.

Seemingly out of nowhere, I had this nagging feeling that if I tell people that I'm enlightened, if I promise people that I can help them create the conditions for rapid enlightenment, that I would be publicly humiliated.

To make things even more fun, my wife Kristen, had the exact same feeling. There is no basis for this feeling. The Drunk Monkey is just raining on our parade, trying to keep us "safe."

I got the inspiration to write this book in January. I'm just getting started, and it's mid-May. It's taken me this long to sort through this Unconscious Reflex.

First off, can we just celebrate how amazing that is? Four and a half months of being stuck!! Wow!! That is nothing in the grand scheme of things.

This book is a life changer for me. Even if only one person reads it, the fact that I took the time to document the process of rapid enlightenment is a personal best. It's a crowning achievement in my life.

How many people die with their book still in them? How many people have the inspiration to do something life-changing and it takes decades to find the courage? Four and a half months is a blip on the time scale of life.

Okay...Stop! Did you see what I just did there? That's Recontextualization in action. It's the skill of describing the conditions and circumstances of your life in a way that empowers you. I snuck that in just to make sure you are getting it. :-)

So how did I do it so fast? There are three parts to the process.

Part One: Distinguish The Unconscious Reflex

Kristen and I were fearful. We both kept getting unwanted visions of being humiliated and our peace being taken from us.

Because we have trained thousands of people and practiced distinguishing The Unconscious Reflexes in our own life, our enlightened alarm bell went off. We were Forecasting The Negative.

Part Two: Distinguish The Hidden Motive To Survive

Every Unconscious Reflex has a trigger. The triggers are programs in consciousness itself. They are like filters. If I put a filter over my camera lens, I'm not seeing things exactly as they are.

Hidden Motives are exactly like that. They distort your reality in an effort to help you survive.

We distinguished that there was a Hidden Motive To Survive distorting our perspective called Traitor. This is the motive to hide who you really are for fear of being negatively affected.

The program seems to be encoded in our consciousness. It's a very deep and almost completely undistinguished motive to survive. So, we used the Traitor release meditation to defuse the impact of this Hidden Motive, and undo the Unconscious Reflex.

I've created release mediations for all ten Hidden Motives To Survive. Download them all at matthewferry.com/motives

Kristen and I would release one aspect of Traitor, feeling like we needed to hide ourselves for fear of negative consequences. Then we would discover that there were other versions. So we just did the release meditation over and over again until all of the Traitor energy was gone.

Concurrently, Kristen and I used The Releasing Attachment exercise (find it in the Appendix). When The Drunk Monkey exaggerates the potential of loss, you become attached to getting the results you seek. The attachment degrades you.

If you don't see the exaggeration for what it is, then you will be fearful for no reason. This clouds your decision-making. It causes you to procrastinate.

In this case, Kristen and I saw that we were attached to our peace. The Drunk Monkey was Forecasting The Negative and telling us that we were going to be discredited and attacked if we taught The Rapid Enlightenment Process publicly.

However, The Drunk Monkey is not psychic. The Drunk Monkey doesn't know what the future holds.

By seeing The Drunk Monkey Forecasting The Negative, removing The Hidden Motive To Survive that got activated, and Releasing Attachment to a certain set of outcomes, I was able to make peace with the fact that what I talk about is disruptive to the spiritual status quo.

Part Three: Create A New Context (Recontextualize)

I accept that my casual demeanor, and "no BS", street-style, matter-of-fact teaching style often agitates people who are desperately seeking enlightenment through their religious traditions. I realize that I tend to offend people. I have my entire life.

If people are uncomfortable and seek to discredit me publicly, then so be it. Kristen and I both possess the tools to remain in an authentic state of joy, peace, flow, and prosperity no matter what happens in the external environment.

We are inspired to bring The Rapid Enlightenment Process into the world, and we appreciate that there will be a broad spectrum of responses. We don't resist all the potential futures that may unfold. Instead we take intentional action on what we are committed to.

That's the context we've created to eliminate the impact of the Unconscious Reflex Forecasting The Negative, and the underlying Hidden Motive To Survive called Traitor.

By now, you are seeing how the Unconscious Reflects of The Drunk Monkey and The Hidden Motives To Survive are linked.

Unwanted Talking In Your Head

I am betting you are confronted by unwanted, unneeded talking in your head that is persuading you to not put yourself at risk of being uncomfortable.

But The Drunk Monkey's perspective is false. The futures that it fears are not real. They are just possibilities. The futures it projects into the theater of your mind assumes you are weak. Nothing could be further from the truth.

In your process of becoming enlightened, your primary job is to challenge The Drunk Monkey at all times. Never take anything your survival mind says at face value.

The Drunk Monkey makes up stories. It estimates. Its motives are *not* your motives. It is concerned with baseline biological drives like looking good to get a mate or being well-regarded to make sure the tribe stays by your side during dangerous circumstances.

If you are reading these words, then you have transcended the basic survival pursuits of being human. You are now fully entrenched in your desire to experience enlightened states.

When The Drunk Monkey is Forecasting The Negative, it is doing its job. It is working to keep you away from potential rejection, embarrassment, harassment, or wasting time.

The Drunk Monkey is attached to looking good, being smart, fitting in, being well-liked, etc.

These are all great survival strategies if you are a pack animal like human beings.

Our ancestors needed to fit in, in order to survive.

As a creative, free-thinking, bold person committed to living Epic Life, you are not in a survival situation. You are in a creative, thriving, prosperous, make-something-new-happen situation.

Anytime you feel like The Drunk Monkey is Forecasting The Negative, use these awareness questions create a new context. Ask yourself:

- How do I know that this is true?
- Where did I learn this?
- Can I tell the future?
- What will really happen if I do this?
- What am I committed to?
- What do I want?

- What is the best possible outcome?

- What is the most effortless action I can take today to get the ball rolling?

- What do I need to say to The Drunk Monkey to make it feel comfortable?

Don't get mad at your mind. Don't turn The Drunk Monkey into an enemy.

The Drunk Monkey has served you and your ancestors well. Forecasting The Negative is very useful when you are taking *actual* risks. If you have the power to see the upside and downside of any given situation, you are better informed. If you can unemotionally weigh the pros and cons, you can make better decisions. This is an amazing biological function.

Where The Drunk Monkey goes off the rails is when you believe that the negative forecast is true and start to feel fearful. It's terrible if you don't have the conscious awareness to recognize that it's a made-up story and it has no basis in reality.

As an enlightened person, you must practice seeing that The Drunk Monkey's negative forecast is just one possibility in a sea of possibilities.

If you get really honest with yourself, you even begin to see that the odds of those negative things happening almost never apply to someone who is creative, free-thinking, bold, and persistent like you.

Once you become aware of that The Drunk Monkey uses the Unconscious Reflex Forecasting The Negative, you can Recontextualize and create a context that empowers you.

Chapter 12
The Desire To Fit In

Awareness of The Drunk Monkey and its Unconscious Reflexes puts you at the height of humanity. When you can spot these aspects of the mind, you will appear to have otherworldly power to transform problems and issues.

As you enlighten, you will naturally move into a trusted advisor role in your community. Your family, friends, and colleagues will flock to you for your counsel. As a result, you will find yourself with lots of new and interesting opportunities.

I have found my clients and students who embrace Enlightened Perspectives are more prosperous, stable, and consistent than others. And by the way, many of my students resisted what I am teaching you. The fact that you are reading this right now is an indicator that you possess a propensity for enlightenment.

To achieve Quiet Mind Epic Life, you must become a master of awareness. Awareness makes you flexible, which reveals new options and gives you power.

Unconscious Reflex: The Desire To Fit In

It is imperative that you start to notice how you are unconsciously driven to fit in. We are each impacted by the familial, cultural and societal influences we are exposed to from a very young age.

From a survival standpoint, it is very valuable to learn how to be a part of a pack. But, from an Enlightened Perspective, you see that this reflex must be transcended.

It's time to be honest with yourself. You and I are pack animals. It is a simple fact that our genetic history is based on the pack mentality. Banding together, for the good of the group, is pervasive in our consciousness.

By forming complex social groups who all work together our species has created a very successful structure for survival.

Each family group is a microcosm of the larger whole. Making sacrifices for the family and putting your needs aside for the greater good of the family, was domesticated into you through a complex system of assumptive language patterns, rewards, and punishments.

From a very early age, you began to mirror the behavior of your family group in order to be accepted as a part of the group and nurtured.

The Unconscious Reflex called The Desire To Fit In is very powerful. Your genes are programmed with the behaviors that developed from times when being an outcast meant death.

As a child, you were compelled to do whatever it took to win your parents' love. Almost everyone (not all) grows up in environments where being yourself meant upsetting the family group. Very few people are able to say what they really think, dress the way they want, live the way they want, and create the life they want without upsetting the people in their life.

I want you to really let this next statement in and ponder it.

Ready?

The odds of you staying aligned with pack mentality while fully self-expressed and living your full potential are damn near zero.

Enlightenment changes all of that.

We celebrate those people who break away from the pack and do something that took courage. It's so rare. So few can escape the gravity of The Desire To Fit In.

I'm not saying that successful people like Oprah and Richard Branson who break the cultural norms are enlightened. But their creative courage represents an ability to ignore the Hidden Motives To Survive and Unconscious Reflexes.

You must catch The Drunk Monkey blinding you with the Unconscious Reflex Desire To Fit In. It causes you to believe that behaving differently is risky.

Think about the story I told you about the fear that this book would cause me to be ostracized in my professional community. That's a cocktail of Motives and Reflexes that could have kept this book from being in your hands right now.

Let's just get practical. When you break protocol with your culture, your business associates, your friend group, or family, they get uncomfortable. They don't even know why. They are slaves to The Drunk Monkey and crave conformity.

When you do what you want, it is disruptive to the status quo.

Oftentimes, if you are brave enough to do what makes you happy, your family and friends will experience a fight or flight response. They want you to keep being exactly who you are, following the unconscious rules that they are following. This helps their Drunk Monkey keep you in a neat and tidy little box.

They are programmed to believe that different is dangerous. This aspect of our survival system was developed hundreds of thousands of years ago. It's how we identify who's in the tribe and who's not. If you behave differently, then you are not part of the pack, which means you might be a threat.

Okay...I know, I know. I hear it. I hear your Drunk Monkey.

"Matthew, I don't want to upset the people in my life. Maybe I don't need this Quiet Mind Epic Life stuff after all. I feel like I should put this book down. Maybe it's too risky."

Hold on there, Skippy.

First of all, it's too late. You can't help yourself. Buddha said it perfectly, "Once one hears of enlightenment, nothing else will do." You have been on this quest for a long time. So just make peace with it. It's been happening your whole life. You've always been different from the rest of the herd.

Secondly, you are just proving my point. You are not free. This reflex to stop seeking enlightenment for fear of not fitting into the group is exactly what I'm trying to free you from. You are having a reaction. I'm just typing words blah blah blah, and you are making up stories about how the people in your life are going to react. My words are the hammer and your thoughts are the knee springing up automatically.

Is that what you are committed to? You want to be a mindless robot programmed by society so as not to ruffle feathers?

Bringing an Enlightened Perspective to your culture, business, friends, and family will be one of the greatest benefits that you could ever bring. There is no greater prize than bringing the example of profound peace to the people in your life. Ultimately, in your enlightened state your presence will be experienced as a gift.

Here's a reminder of what's at stake.

Enlightenment provides you with a context to enjoy unbelievable freedom, creativity, power, and influence over your life. As you pierce through the veil of the mind's denial system, you will have more power over your life. When you see life as innocent, perfect, or meaningless, you deal with things much more sensibly.

When you embrace your Enlightened Perspective, there is no suffering. There is no desire. There is no worry. There is no doubt. There is bold creative energy. There is inspiration. There is just love, compassion, and acceptance for all. The joy you will feel is so overwhelming that you will burst into tears of joy on a regular basis; you will be grateful to be alive.

You want that, right?

It is the most delicious state you can possibly imagine. You are on the verge of that right now. I've given you my word. Hold me to it.

So let's quiet The Drunk Monkey together. I've got your back.

At first, your unwillingness to participate in gossip, your release of negative attitudes, your unbridled compassion, and your willingness to accept everyone for everything they represent will be very disruptive to the people you know.

They are used to you being jealous, agitated, judgmental, prideful, playing the victim, and excluding people who aren't in the group. Yes, even you, the kind and loving spirit that you are can be mad, frustrated and righteous. I know who I am talking to.

As you release your need to fit in and toe the family line, your joy will start to burst out of you. The good news is, your joy will be very attractive to the majority of people in your life. Some of the Negative Nellies won't like you anymore. But I'm pretty sure you are okay with letting the Negative Nellies go, right?

In the past, you have been naturally drawn to activities and behaviors that are consistent with the way you were raised and the people you associate with.

Most families do not have a culture of enlightenment. For most families, practicing total and complete acceptance of all people in all situations is thought of as dangerous.

You were likely told to exclude people who aren't "The Right Kind of People".

You were conditioned to believe that gossip, negativity, and being judgmental are normal. You may have felt that if you didn't participate, then you were in opposition to your family members.

Survival programs are very different than an enlightened consciousness. Your family group did the right thing. They did their best to show you how to live in the world. They were not concerned with happiness and peace. They were concerned with you being able to put food on the table, find a mate, have babies and keep the species alive. You were taught survival.

Let's look at how The Desire to Fit In takes us out of alignment with ourselves and what to do about it.

My client Sally (name changed to keep our confidentiality agreement), is a mom of three great kids. She comes from an upper-middle-class family. She's been married to the same man for coming up on two decades. He is very, very successful and has very strong opinions on most things.

Sally is easygoing. She likes quiet time. She is very intuitive. Most would people would say she is a sensitive soul. Like you and I, she is deeply spiritual.

When we met, she was a long way from enlightenment. She was in those beginning stages where you know how to be happy but so many things knock you off your center. It took consistently engaging The Rapid Enlightenment Process to go into enlightened states, but eventually, she got there.

One of the biggest blocks to her joy was the unconscious pull to fit in. She wanted to be a great mom. She wanted to do well by her children.

But what she was sure made her a "good mom" caused her lots of suffering and lamenting. She was incessantly worried about living life "the right way" fearing if she didn't her kids would be screwed up because of her. She couldn't stand the idea that they would have bad lives because of her.

If you are a parent, I know you can relate to this story.

Using awareness exercises, hours of reflection, and self-examination, Sally began to see that she was being run around like a dog on a leash by The Drunk Monkey.

Step One: Distinguish The Unconscious Reflex

Sally's inner conflict was fueled by The Desire To Fit In. As she pondered changing her rules, it filled her with anxiety. It surprised her. She became present to her Unconscious Reflex to fit in. Making herself happy and doing what she thought was right caused her fight or flight mechanism to fire off.

"What will my husband think? What will my parents think? Will my friends think I'm a bad mom because I break with tradition and follow my heart?"

She just kept noticing her body's reaction. Her heart rate went up. She became filled with anxiety. The Drunk Monkey had her in its grips.

Now you know that at the heart of every Unconscious Reflex is a Hidden Motive To Survive. In this case, Sally began to distinguish that she was compelled to follow a set of rules about child rearing that she never consciously chose.

Step Two: Distinguish The Hidden Motive

On investigation, Sally was able to discern that the Hidden Motive To Survive called Illogical Rules at work. Remember there are 10 motives that pervade our consciousness. They aren't mental. They are actually energetic. They are the cause that gets The Drunk Monkey talking.

Illogical Rules were the source of Sally's conflict. She did some journaling and made a list of rules that you, "have to follow" if you are going to be a good parent.

Almost immediately, she discovered these rules didn't make her feel good. She was surprised and didn't even know where they came from.

She noticed that following these Illogical Rules for being a good parent were ingrained in her. She noticed that her husband adhered to them too. She reflected on her childhood and saw that even her mom and dad demonstrated these rules in how they raised her.

Her journal list was filled with the telltale signs of Illogical Rules: have to, need to, must, should, and shouldn't. So many of the rules conflicted with what she actually believed. The conflict inside of her became very clear.

Remember that awareness is the critical first step.

To undo The Drunk Monkey's grip, Sally devoted herself to bringing an Enlightened Perspective to her process. She started by doing the Release Illogical Rules release meditation over and over again. (Find all the Hidden Motive Release Meditations at- matthewferry.com/motives)

Sally's objective was to heal this newly discovered distortion in her consciousness. She wanted to release the irrational filter created by the Hidden Motive to Follow Illogical Rules. She wanted to literally remove its energy signature from her consciousness.

Next, she confronted The Drunk Monkey using a Recontextualization tool called The Worst Case Scenario. (See the Appendix for a step-by-step guide.)

Sally used her intentional creative mind to play out the worst possible scenario if she were to follow her heart and raise her kids the way she wanted to.

The Drunk Monkey already has a powerful ability to use imagination to Forecast The Negative. In this exercise, Sally used her powerful imagination to look at the worst, most nasty outcomes. Once she completed the Worst Case Scenario exercise, a strange and pervasive peace came over Sally. She didn't want the worst to happen. But she had put The Drunk Monkey's fears to the test and come up with a plan *if* the worst happened.

Seeing how the Unconscious Reflex Desire To Fit In was being caused by the Hidden Motive To Survive Illogical Rules gave Sally a new awareness. With that awareness, she was able to apply the Worst Case Scenario exercise and shift her context.

This awareness freed her from survival-based consciousness and made way for Enlightened Perspectives to influence how she wants to raise her kids. Sally is now at peace. She's happy. She's no longer impacted by a Hidden Motive triggering an Unconscious Reflex when it comes to parenting.

Now Sally has mind-bending power to create her epic life as a mom.

. . . .

The survival mind has a profound desire to fit in and stay with the pack. To The Drunk Monkey, the prospect of going against the status quo is a risk, so it responds with fear, anxiety, doubt, and worry.

. . . .

Where are is the Unconscious Reflex Desire To Fit In impacting you?

Chapter 13
Holding Others Accountable To Agreements They Never Made

You want Quiet Mind Epic Life?

Then you will have to practice awareness of The Drunk Monkey and its Unconscious Reflexes over and over again.

In other words, you are going to experience a quantum leap in your happiness and peace the first time you go through this process. Your life will get really good, really fast.

But that's not the end. That's just the beginning. Can you imagine going to the gym once and expecting to be fit the rest of your life? It doesn't work that way.

An Enlightened Perspective is a skill set you must continue to practice to maintain it in your life.

Diets typically don't work because they aren't intended to be a way of living.

However, experiencing Enlightened Perspectives *is* intended to be a way of living in the modern world. Unless you are planning on spending your time holed up in a cave somewhere totally cut off from society, you will have Hidden Motives To Survive triggering Unconscious Reflexes. That's why you will use the tools I'm giving you for the rest of your life.

Look, suffering is normal. Happiness is weird. You are going to be the odd one out when you take on these practices. That's why Kristen and I have created a community of like-minded people who all hang out and help each other practice living with Enlightened Perspectives.

Ready for the next stop on our Drunk Monkey tour? Let me introduce you to the Unconscious Reflex Holding People Accountable To Agreements They Never Made.

What The Drunk Monkey Thinks

The Drunk Monkey believes that all other people should behave the way you behave. The Drunk Monkey cannot recognize that it was programmed to behave the way it does. It does not consider that it believes what it does because of your family, community, and culture.

It thinks that what it thinks is what everyone else should think. (That's a tongue twister!)

The Drunk Monkey is naive. Yet, you listen to it like an all-knowing sage.

Here's a perfect example. When your friend tells you how she dealt with a work situation, The Drunk Monkey instantaneously makes her wrong. Without skipping a beat, it jumps in and says, "If I was you, I would have done XYZ. Why didn't you do that?"

Your friend looks at you and wonders why you've gone from ally to enemy.

A client calls your vendor and asks about a product you sell. You go ballistic! "How dare she do that to me! She went around my back! She has no right!"

Let's tear it apart. In the client's mind, calling the vendor was the proper thing to do. Unless you specifically said, "under no circumstance are you to call my vendor." In very few cases that is true. In almost all cases, you expected your client to behave the way you would behave.

Instead of seeing things from their point of view, you think, "How could they do that to me? Boohoo. I'm a victim, boohoo. Feel sorry for me, boohoo. I have no power, boohoo. I have been violated, boohoo." What does all of that Drunk Monkey posturing really mean? It means that you learned early on in life to be a victim (Hidden Motive To Survive alert!) to get people's sympathy and attention. And here you are, an adult still doing the same thing. Eek!

Let's be honest. Your client didn't violate you. You violated yourself with your unexamined reaction. Your reaction did the damage to you. You were holding your client accountable to an agreement they didn't make.

When *The Drunk Monkey* is holding others accountable to agreements they never made it just gets mean. It mentally beats people up for not doing things the way it thinks they should.

Your Expectations Were Broken

Any time your expectations are broken, you have to ask yourself, "Did they specifically agree to this expectation or am I holding them to an agreement they never made?"

If they agreed, then you have a leg to stand on. With awareness, you will be shocked at how often you are angry at someone for not doing something they didn't agree to.

The Drunk Monkey literally thinks things like, "Matthew! Don't be stupid! It's obvious to everyone that you do ABC when you encounter XYZ."

The Drunk Monkey is arrogant, which means it's ignorant. What is obvious to you may be a mystery to someone else. What makes perfect sense to you may be completely insane to someone else.

You are not the ruler of the universe. But, if you pay attention to The Drunk Money, you will discover that The Drunk Monkey believes that you are.

If you don't catch The Drunk Monkey using this Unconscious Reflex, then you are destined to live a life of broken expectations, blow-ups, and feeling like a victim.

When people don't behave the way you do, they become suspects. The Drunk Monkey is not able to put them in the nice and tidy "safe" box. When people behave outside of your expectations, the Drunk Monkey puts them in the "potential threat" box. It goes on high alert. Its fight or flight mechanism gets activated.

You will not be able to maintain enlightened consciousness when your fight or flight is activated. Your consciousness will be focused on lower-level concerns like staying safe, being right, maintaining control, getting your way, proving you are right, seeking revenge, and making sure people know you are important.

This guarantees suffering. Not suffering like prolonged anguish. Suffering like never feeling quite right within yourself. Never being totally satisfied. Never feeling like you are in the right place at the right time. Feeling like you need to change things to be happy. For a fairly high-conscious person, that is what suffering looks like.

Because you are high-conscious, you are used to getting your way. So, when people don't do what you want them to do and break your expectations, you are used to manipulating them into compliance. But this robs you of your joy. To exert force and will people to your point of view, means you are pushing against something. This tendency to harbor silent expectations will always create a counter-force pushing back at you. That makes your life harder and robs you of your inner joy.

From an Enlightened Perspective, the goal is to experience life as easy, effortless, flowing, and enjoyable.

Here are six awareness exercises that neutralize Holding People Accountable to Agreements They Never Made.

1. Nobody signed up for your way of living life. Everyone was raised by different people. Your way is not more right or wrong than anyone else's way.

2. No one named you the ruler of the universe. No one appointed you to The Code of Conduct Police. Your rules for how people are supposed to behave, talk, walk, dress, and conduct business are just a set of preferences that you have. Your preferences are not the truth. They are not best, and they are not even valid. They are what works for you.

3. Where did your rules of conduct come from? Did you make them up? NO!! You adopted them from observ-

ing the people in your early formative years. You were domesticated like an animal. You probably barely even know what your rules are. You only know when they aren't being followed.

4. What makes your philosophy on life more right than someone else's? Why you? Are you the model of good behavior? Was Jesus more right than Buddha? Was Muhammad more right then Krishna? No. They are all perfect for the people who benefit from their message. You are not the Messiah. No one cares what you think.

    By the way, I'm not the Messiah either. No one cares what I think. Based on how far you are into this book, I suspect you and I are aligned in some ways in our thinking.

    But that doesn't give me a right to get mad at you if you don't follow the system I'm outlining in this book. :-)

5. Your opinion is the source of your suffering, not how other people behave. What you say about it causes you to suffer. Other people are just doing what they are doing. Your resistance causes your suffering, not the circumstances.

    Here's what is currently happening. A person does something that breaks your expectations. You label it as bad or wrong or not good. Your label makes you feel bad. Then, you stupidly blame them for your suffering. It's stupid because you are the only one who can create peace, harmony, and joy in your human experience. By blaming them, you give that power away.

6. People are doing the best they can based on their perspective at the moment. We are all burdened with an ineffective perception of the world. We each do our best to live an enjoyable life using the filters we have.

Give people a little grace to step on cow pies. You aren't the model of perfection. Don't expect other people to be perfect either.

Lastly, if everyone did what you did and felt the way that you felt, this would be a very boring life.

Let's look at five new options to create Quiet Mind Epic Life.

1. Hold people accountable to what they actually commit to. Don't hold people to the imaginary rules you have imposed on them.

2. Put yourself in their shoes. Rather than react, look at the world through their eyes. Practice noticing that they act correctly based on their point of view.

3. Let people off the hook, and forgive them for not knowing your code of conduct. They are doing the best they can based on the way they see the world.

4. Practice recognizing that you don't know everything. Embrace the infinite mystery of being human. Be willing to admit you don't know how life is supposed to be. Practice being curious rather than arrogant.

5. Practice total and complete acceptance of all people, in all situations, at all times; including yourself. What you accept will transform. What you resist will persist. When you accept someone exactly as they are, the things that bug you about them seem to disappear right before your eyes.

Chapter 14
Avoid Making The Same Mistake Twice

Okay, I know I'm overly enthusiastic about Quiet Mind Epic Life and living with Enlightened Perspectives. That's because it's so awesome!

During the last two days, Kristen and I had a breakdown over money. This was mostly because I was irresponsible (which is true) and that she had to clean up my messes (which is also true).

It's been about a 24-hour period with no peace of mind. We have both been on a roller coaster. We have been going through various states of being disgruntled, having little temper tantrums, and blaming on both sides. Definitely not Quiet Mind Epic Life.

Here's the amazing part. We both have the tools to go within, reflect on what causes our upset, and then release it.

This all happened between Tuesday at 10am to Wednesday at 10am. Twenty-four short hours! Do you know how amazing that is?

I was irresponsible. It created a blow-up. She was mad. I was proud. She was a victim. I was being annoyed. She was resentful. Sounds like marriage, right?

Here's the difference. She took the time to uncover what her reaction was and released it. I took the time to uncover what was at the source of my irresponsible behavior.

Bam! The breakthrough begins to happen within 24 hours! That's crazy good!

Financial turmoil (and how you deal with it) is the kind of thing that can shake a marriage to the core. Using the tools in this book not only helped us move past the upset quickly, but we are now in the process of becoming even more financially strong as a couple. The breakdown has started a breakthrough.

You may be asking what the result has been. Well, today we were sitting in the backyard, and my mind was so quiet that I was overwhelmed by the beauty of the trees, butterflies, and birds. Optimism has returned.

This is how life is. It's messy. The Drunk Monkey is irrational and irresponsible, it holds people accountable to things, it gets mad, and it plays the victim.

The Drunk Monkey is Outdated Software

The Drunk Monkey is an amazing tool for survival. You and I are so lucky to have one. It's not a bad thing. It's the cornerstone of our species' success. Unfortunately, life has changed faster than our biology can keep up with.

The Drunk Monkey is out-of-date software.

Today you are safer than all of your ancestors put together. You are barely ever in real danger. If you have one brush with death in this lifetime, it would be a really big deal.

Be honest, what kills most people these days? What we eat! Ha! But The Drunk Monkey is no help there!

The Drunk Monkey is hard-wired for real danger. Not self-inflicted danger like eating foods that can lead to heart attacks and cancer.

The Drunk Monkey is designed to deal with living in low-conscious, lawless groups of selfish people. Places where there is real danger from animals, work, and other threatening people. But that's likely not you.

You are living at the height of humanity, in one of the safest and most prosperous times in the history of our species.

Is This Time Really Like Last Time?

The Drunk Monkey steers you away from bad things by imagining what *might* happen. It tries to premeditate the outcome. It uses past experiences to determine how to handle present situations.

For example, picture this: you walk down the street and bang yourself up in a fall. The Drunk Monkey will remember that section of the street, and every time you walk down it, you will get a flash of that fall. Pretty awesome, right?

Yes. Awesome for real danger. Terrible for real life. Why?

The Drunk Monkey oversteps its bounds by creating unrelated connections between things.

For example, as a kid, a man in a black overcoat scared you. Now, you are a 30-year-old, and a potential client shows up to a meeting in a black overcoat. You don't know why you feel uncomfortable, but you do. The imbalance in your emotions causes you to present poorly, and the meeting is a bust.

In essence, The Drunk Monkey was left unchecked and correlated a black overcoat to the potential for getting scared.

The Drunk Monkey misunderstands the current situation and shoots your body full of adrenaline - the same biological response from when you were scared as a kid.

For people like you and me, it's very subtle. But instead of using your cognitive, creative, intuitive brain, The Drunk Monkey goes into survival-mode when being optimistic, and resourceful were appropriate.

In this case, you are being impacted by the Unconscious Reflex Avoid Making The Same Mistake Twice. The Drunk Monkey assumes, "last time this happened, so that means this time it will happen too." Of course, this rationale is insane.

Can you imagine saying to your child, "Look, the last time you tried to walk, you kept falling down. This walking thing doesn't seem to work for you. Just crawl around for the rest of your life."

That's what The Drunk Monkey is proposing to you on a regular basis. It tries to convince you this time will be like last time. It wants you to avoid making the same mistake twice.

Awareness makes you flexible, which reveals new options to give you the power to decide what you're committed to. The power to shape your destiny.

As a side note, having an Enlightened Perspective doesn't solve your inadequacies. For example, if you are undisciplined with money, your Enlightened Perspective won't make you more disciplined. It won't magically solve all of your problems. It *will* give you the personal power to address your inadequacies with peace, joy, and bold intensity. You will become unburdened by insecurity and self-deprecation.

The Drunk Monkey uses its forecasting ability to see if "this time" is like that "other time" in the past.

Rather than being specific and exact, The Drunk Monkey relies on generalization. It approximates. It fills in the gaps. It assumes. With introspection, you realize that The Drunk Monkey inaccurately assesses the situation most of the time.

The Drunk Monkey says, "Don't make that call. Last time you asked her for something, she told you no. She will tell you no again."

But this time is not like last time. So many variables have changed. The Drunk Monkey collapses all of its information together and presents it to you like its assessment is a sure thing.

The Drunk Monkey says, "I'm not a big fan of snowboarding. The last time you went snowboarding, you fell on your ass and your tailbone was sore for days."

Rather than addressing the basic premise of learning (aka failing over and over until you succeed), The Drunk Monkey categorically rules out mistakes as a vital part of any journey.

· · · · · · · · · · · · · · · · · · · ·

The Drunk Monkey steers you away from bad things by imagining what might happen. It uses past experiences to determine how to handle present situations.

· · · · · · · · · · · · · · · · · · · ·

Don't Live Your Life Trying to Avoid Making Mistakes

1. It's a mistake NOT to make mistakes. There is no failure. There is only learning. Mistakes and failure are the paths to getting the new things you want in your life. You don't discourage your kid to stop trying to catch the ball because she keeps dropping it. Don't stop going after what you want because you haven't achieved it yet.

2. Create a new context to empower yourself when you are afraid of making the same mistake twice. Write a short script that you will say to The Drunk Monkey to help it feel safe in the moment.

   You are going to have to learn how to talk to The Drunk Monkey like it is separate from you.

   Maybe you will say, "Everything I do is perfect no matter what the results are. I love being uncomfortable because it means I'm doing something new. New actions mean new results. Let's do an experiment and see what happens. Let's find out who's right."

When you spot The Drunk Monkey trying to Avoid Making The Same Mistake Twice, neutralize this Unconscious Reflex by taking action anyway.

Chapter 15
Following Rules That Don't Exist

The more you accept, the less you resist. The less you resist, the happier you are. The happier you are, the easier it is to think, express, create, etc.

When you are happy, you are more resourceful. You are easier to deal with. This gives you an unbelievably strategic advantage in your life.

The Unconscious Reflexes of The Drunk Monkey are operating in the background and nearly invisible to most people. If you are unable to see them distorting your point of view and ruining your experience, then you will be stuck in a life of persistent dissatisfaction.

For someone like you, it's subtle, but it's there. You are already on your way to enlightenment. You have already been addressing the issues standing in the way of living with a quiet mind.

Your version of dissatisfaction is likely more subtle than the people around you. You know that I am talking about. For the most part, your life works. You are in a good place. But small stuff still takes you out. You still secretly wish people and situations were different. And you don't know what to do about it.

That's why you are reading this book. In a truly enlightened state, this book is irrelevant because you will be living in a state of persistent happiness, joy, peace, and satisfaction. That's epic.

You ready to continue?

Let's tackle the next Unconscious Reflex called Following Rules The Don't Exist. This one is a game-changer on your path to becoming truly free.

To begin, I have a question. How did you become the person you are today? The simple answer is simple: Conditioning.

When you came out of the womb, you were innocent, fresh, unexposed, unspoiled, and basically pure potential. And I am betting you were darn cute too!

The people who raised you instinctively knew this innocence in you. And thankfully, they were driven by their programming to do their best to help you become a fully functioning adult.

Slowly but surely, they indoctrinated you into a belief system that includes: how to talk, dress, act, think, move, sleep, when to wake up, what's right, wrong, good, bad, etc.

Every single aspect of your personality and behavior is a function of the environment you grew up in and the relationship you had to it.

Another way to put it: You didn't actually choose who you are. Your context, beliefs, and corresponding behavior was the result of your conditioning.

I know this is not anything new to you. To be able to hang in this conversation, you have to have a baseline knowledge of popular psychology.

Yet, I'm certain you are blind to the rules you follow that are in conflict with achieving Quiet Mind Epic Life. You blindly follow rules of protocol, and in many cases, they contradict your desire for peace.

The Drunk Monkey follows a list of rules and protocols that it believes will keep you safe and ensure you maintain the status quo.

In your professional life, you might find yourself conflicted by reaching out to prospective clients and asking them to work with you. You get stopped by an unexamined rule programmed into your consciousness that says, "Don't be pushy."

In some ways, this is very practical. As a kid, your parents were doing their best to teach you good social skills. However, if you were constantly trying to manipulate them to get your way, then they may have responded with consistent pushback until they got you back in line. I do this with my 10-year-old when he asks for a cookie eight times in a row.

Now you are forty years old and paralyzed by the thought of asking someone you don't know for something. You are afraid they will push back and not give you what you want, so you don't dare ask.

Once you start operating from an Enlightened Perspective, your ability to discern rules that don't exist is greatly enhanced. You will naturally start asking yourself, "Why am I doing it this way? Who said it has to be like this? Where did I learn this? Why am I making it so hard on myself? Is this limitation real?"

Awareness is the key. Awareness makes you flexible, which reveals new options and gives you power.

Remember Unconscious Reflexes of The Drunk Monkey are fueled by Hidden Motives To Survive.

I have a client who is still struggling to get his business as profitable as he wants after years of trying. On investigation we were able to discern he was unwilling to admit he was following a rule that didn't exist. His rule was based on the Hidden Motive To Survive called Greed. He'd say "If I offer profit sharing to my key people, then there won't be enough for me". His company struggles to grow because he can't get A players to buy into his business model. The Drunk Monkey has the upper hand.

Another client had a rule that she had to be there physically with her children no matter what. This created marital problems because she refused to let anyone else watch her children. Her husband begged her for alone time, but she couldn't escape the Hidden Motive To Survive Pride that confirmed she was the only one worthy of watching her children.

I encourage you to use The Rule Breaker Questions on the following page to examine all the rules that you are blindly following.

Ghandi said, "Thus the basis of integrity is a destinal resolve - a resolve that chooses and sets your destiny and out of which your whole life is ordered. The object of that resolve is the ultimate decision of each person, and each person makes that choice, consciously or unconsciously. To do so with awareness is the height of man's responsibility. It is incarnate freedom. It is what real freedom looks like. When man has thus exercised his freedom he realizes that to be true to himself ever thereafter he has a unique position to look at the values of his society. He is no longer bound by the opinions and codes of his fellow-man, but reevaluates them on the basis of their impact on his destinal resolve."

Kierkegaard said, "Know yourself, and to your own self, be true."

It's Time To Discover The Rules

As a seeker of Enlightened Perspective, it's time to discover the rules that you have been following blindly. Begin to see the rules that have trapped you in a prison of your own making.

This doesn't give you permission to start breaking all the rules. That would be very disruptive to the people around you. When the people around you are disturbed by you, it is difficult to create a quiet mind. You are going to have to use your discernment. You are going to learn, through failure, to be very polite and graceful in your exit from societal programming.

Breaking rules that don't exist does not give you permission to unilaterally break your word. I am not suggesting that you become an irresponsible jerk on your way to Quiet Mind Epic Life. I am suggesting there are likely hundreds of agreements that you have made that have integrity for the relationship of both parties but lack integrity for you. If you decide to 'break' these rules, I request you do it with integrity and grace.

Your objective is to slowly, gently, and respectfully, break the rules that don't exist in reality.

Rules are easy to spot because they hold you back. They cause you to react. They keep valuable action, activities, and behaviors just out of reach.

When you spot a rule that isn't serving you, use The Rule Breaker Questions:

- Is this reaction moving me in the direction of Quiet Mind Epic Life?
- What is the hidden benefit of my reaction?
- To what am I actually committed?
- What rule is getting violated?

- What is the negative impact of this rule?

- Where did this rule come from?

Now, rewrite the rule to make sure you can respond, be empowered, and enjoy a Quiet Mind Epic Life.

Chapter 16
Avoiding Failure

To be enlightened is a rare thing indeed. It takes a tremendous commitment to look within. As you adopt more and more Enlightened Perspectives, you are going to face the gravity of leaving your old life. If you stay within your old life's confines, it is going to pull you back to playing the victim, getting frustrated, and going into down cycles over and over on your journey.

Awareness of the Unconscious Reflexes is critical. The more you study this material, the quieter your mind will become. With a quiet mind, you will start to have deep and profound insights into the nature of your existence.

Spiritual texts that seemed cryptic before will become completely obvious to you. Mental blocks that used to plague your existence will melt away. You will be dumbstruck by the beauty of the world.

When you were burdened by the mind and its distorted reality, you looked at the black widow spider, and maybe you saw a negative creature. However, in your enlightened state, you see the beauty and the perfection of its existence within the whole of the universe.

That's a sweet spot to be in. From that perspective, you are creative and free. When you have the burden of a survival-based mind, you are restricted and limited. When you transcend survival based thinking, you enter into a new realm of experience and existence.

Awareness is the key to it all. You must learn to spot the Unconscious Reflexes driving your behavior in order to transcend the mind's motives for thinking.

Failure Is Not Bad

The Drunk Monkey is afraid that failure means something bad about you personally. It fears embarrassment. It believes that the failure to accomplish what you set out to do will signify that something is wrong with you.

With awareness, you begin to discover that The Drunk Monkey is afraid that you are not good enough, you are not smart enough, or maybe, that you are too shy. There is a long list of what it is afraid of. It might be afraid that you are ugly, not pretty, not worthy of love, not worthy of attention. We each have our own cocktail of Drunk Monkey insanity.

Reading this book is evidence that you are a free-thinking individual who is striving to experience peace and joy. You are not satisfied with the status quo. You don't believe that you are limited by the circumstances you were born into. You believe that you are destined for an epic life.

You have probably achieved a lot in your life already. You have likely explored the impact of being successful, making money, and even being popular.

Yet, you know there is more. You have an unexplainable pull to go farther, improve, push, and create.

I've worked with some of the most successful people in the world. Billionaires, gold medalists, Grammy Award winners, and the like. People with professional accomplishments and academic degrees that would make your head spin. They are all still burdened by The Drunk Monkey's Unconscious Reflex Avoiding Failure.

Here are some of the statements these ultra-successful people have shared with me in the past:

- "I'm afraid that my clients will think I'm an idiot."
- "I don't want to be embarrassed."
- "What if it doesn't work and I go broke?
- "I don't want to get fired."
- "I will be laughed at."
- "What will others think about me?"
- "I don't want to look stupid."
- "I can't let my family down."

Failure is just learning. It's just a perspective. Failure is the first part of learning and the process you go through to figure things out. (How many times did you "fail" to stand up, on your quest to walk?)

Yet, The Drunk Monkey makes failure mean something bad about you that threatens your status as a member of society.

Haven't you had enough? Enough about your status in society already! To achieve Quiet Mind Epic Life, you must create the conditions for Enlightened Perspectives. You must renounce your devotion to looking good to society.

That doesn't mean you are going to go live in a cave. It means you are going to rise above the illogical position that you need society's approval for anything.

If you simply step back and look at some of the most successful people in the world, they play by their own rules. They don't do things to impress others as much as they do what is effective to achieve their creative visions and dreams.

BTW, some successful people are destructive in nature, some are constructive. As a high-conscious person, being constructive (uplifting, gracious) is a far more efficient way to get what you want. This is why when you - a high-conscious person - aligns with survival based thinking, you are degraded and you malfunction.

When The Drunk Monkey starts Avoiding Failure, you become rigid and inflexible. You become limited. You become unwilling to try new things. You become stuck in a rut.

The Drunk Monkey is not your friend. It's not on your side. It doesn't want you to change things. It wants to maintain the status quo.

However, it does have a job to do. It wants to steer you away from negative experiences and towards positive ones. *If your visions, dreams, goals, and inspirations create the potential to feel bad, fail, or be embarrassed, it will unconsciously push you to do something else.*

Using your Enlightened Perspective, you ignore The Drunk Monkey's irrelevant warnings and take actions consistent with your true desires.

The Drunk Monkey is similar to a deer eating grass in a field. It looks calm, but it's on high alert at all times. If it senses danger it hits the eject button and runs to safety.

When The Drunk Monkey senses danger for you, you are filled with emotions like stress, frustration, anxiety, anger, and fear.

By now, I don't have to tell you that those emotions degrade your experiences. When fight or flight is engaged, you are not at your best, you don't think straight, and you are not very easy to deal with. The people around you respond poorly to your stress response. It doesn't invoke harmony or cooperation.

Avoiding Failure is actually avoiding a made-up story in your head. Nothing has actually happened yet, but you are reacting like it is definitely going to happen. Suddenly, you are fearful

and insecure. This leads to very destructive behaviors based on pride, arrogance, and being overly aggressive.

••••••••••••••••••••••

When The Drunk Monkey starts Avoiding Failure, you are protecting yourself from a future that isn't here. Joy and inspiration are replaced by fear and force.

••••••••••••••••••••••

To the survival mind, these seem like productive responses to the situation at hand. However, they are all sourced in fear. Fear is degrading.

When your brain chemistry experiences a fight or flight instinct, you don't have access to rational, creative, logical thinking. This massively reduces your effectiveness.

Many of my private coaching clients came to me already very successful people who learned how to thrive in environments where being forceful, arrogant, proud, demanding, and fighting are how you make things happen.

As a result, they are successful AND exhausted. They weren't satisfied with what they had accomplished. They felt like they were the underdog who leads a disadvantaged life. They felt like everything was a game, and they had to win. They Avoided Failure at all cost. As result, they made enemies. People wished them ill wish. Getting things done took tremendous effort.

With an understanding of The Drunk Monkey and its Unconscious Reflexes, today those exact same people are invigorated by their enlightened approach to life. They are satisfied with what they have accomplished, and they are eager to accomplish more. They are unattached to the outcomes. They have a new context for what "failure" means to them and their experience. They have advocates, supporters, and allies. They are collaborative and creative. As a result, many are even MORE successful than before. But, that's not what they care about. They care about maintaining a quiet mind state.

Quiet mind is an indication that you've replaced fear and force with joy and inspiration.

I will say this to you over and over again. You and I are pack animals. In order to survive, our ancestors had to fit in and be a part of the group. We simply don't have to.

To enlighten, you must look past your mind's illusions and stories about failure. Avoiding Failure is the fear of embarrassment, not looking good, or feeling stupid.

The Drunk Monkey avoids failure and distracts you with what is comfortable and safe.

Ironically, The Drunk Monkey's avoidance of failure is the number one cause of failure. Avoiding Failure guarantees failure.

Take a moment now, and see where in your life you are Avoiding Failure, look for the underlying Hidden Motive and listen to the corresponding release meditation found atmatthewferry.com/motives

Can you imagine how much easier life is when you are free of this Unconscious Reflex?

OK, we are almost there. Only one more Unconscious Reflex left.

Now its time to see where The Drunk Monkey's Opinions On Everything is blocking you from experiencing a quiet mind.

Let's go.

Chapter 17
Opinions On Everything

The Drunk Monkey has an opinion on everything. Have you ever been waiting in line at the grocery store, looked at the magazine rack and listened to your mind say, "she's a witch," "what a joke," or, "people are so stupid"?

There you are, minding your own business, and The Drunk Monkey is compelled to weigh in with some random, factless comment like it's the truth. It's insidious.

••

To The Drunk Monkey acting like an authority is essential. It accidentally operates like it has to know everything, as a matter of survival within the pack.

••

It feels like it must be familiar with the details of politics, religion, social protocols, dieting tips, and even the best practices for feeding a child so it can share its perspective at the drop of a hat. Regardless of the topic, your mind will instantly jump into action and start spewing its opinions unasked.

No one is safe.

In fact, The Drunk Monkey will weigh in on anything it is presented with. It has opinions on everything and everyone. Even things it has no knowledge of. It forecasts. It estimates. It assumes.

What few people ever realize is the cost of their opinions. They never take the time notice that the habit of sharing opinions is the source of many arguments. In the end, opinions have very little value and are a main source of your suffering.

In a nutshell, strongly held opinions automatically put you either for something and against something else. They position you in a way that causes you to either be aligned or misaligned with other people. And this is a huge problem (in my opinion-ha!).

Actually, having opinions is not a problem. But, it is an obstacle for one simple reason: opinions rob you of your quiet mind. There is no peace in a mind that is constantly forming, sharing, adjusting, and defending its opinions.

In fact, the unmonitored, ongoing habit of indulging one's opinions as if they are real and valuable, is an enormous waste of time and energy.

Somehow, we've all been taught to believe that our opinions matter. That, without them, we have no place in society, no value in our profession, no status in our family. It leaves us to think that we offer no value, intellect, or connection to "the real world" if we aren't participating by sharing our opinions.

I am here to tell you that this is complete crap. People confuse opinion with preference. They relate to opinions like valued assets that they must propagate, nurture, and grow.

One with strong opinions might think, "The more people who know my opinions, the better. My strong opinions will lead to more power, influence, and success." Wrong.

Opinions are like thieves.

- They steal your quiet mind.
- They repel people.
- They distract you from what's really important and valuable.
- They rob you of enjoying the present moment.
- They block your big dreams from coming true.

To create Quiet Mind Epic Life, you will need to practice applying Enlightened Perspectives to the way in which you engage the world and be honest about what you know and what you don't know.

You must let go of your assumptions. These are just flimsy attempts at trying to understand what's happening so you can look smart, be a part of the conversation, or just feel safe because you think you know something that could connect you to more powerful people.

I request you run an experiment and count how many times a day The Drunk Monkey literally spews an unwanted, uninvited opinion - either as a passing thought or aloud to someone else.

For one day, just notice and count.

I think you'll be inspired to find the Hidden Motives behind this Unconscious Reflex, and take action to neutralize it.

The more you recognize that the source of life within you is the source of life in everyone and everything else and that we are all one thing expressing itself with infinite variety, the more you see the perfection of it all, and the less The Drunk Monkey has to say about it.

Chapter 18
Spotting The Hidden Motives To Survive

Quiet mind really just means that nothing disrupts you. You are balanced. Your physical body, emotions, mind, and soul are all undisturbed. You are balanced.

In this state, nothing causes The Drunk Monkey to talk. The mind is silent. Its motive for talking has been removed. You are at peace.

In this state, there is nothing making you feel uncomfortable in any way. You are finally at home. You are here. You are right now. You are in the present moment. No doubt. No fear. No concern. Nothing more to gain. Nothing to achieve. Nothing to accomplish. No one to impress. Nothing to think about. Nothing to strategize about.

In this state, all is well in your world. You are free from the nagging attachments of desire. You are free from the uncomfortable feelings caused by the illusion that something needs to be fixed. You are free from the illusion that life is incomplete in any way.

Sounds awesome, right?

How do you get there?

It starts with awareness. The purpose of this book is to make you aware. Remember Awareness makes you flexible; which reveals new options and that gives you power.

You are robbed of your quiet mind when the Hidden Motives To Survive are present. In effect, there is an imbalance in your consciousness. The Hidden Motives To Survive cause you to get off center. When you are off center, the mind starts talking.

There is a real reason that enlightened people tend to leave the hustle and bustle of society. They are sensitive to the survival mind and the Hidden Motives behind it.

It takes a very skilled and awake person to be at a family holiday party and not get triggered by the energy that is ping-ponging back and forth between the attendees.

Your history with your family members triggers you into greed, grudge, victim, and a wide variety of motives that put The Drunk Monkey in action.

The interactions between you and your family members (and the subsequent energy that gets activated) blinds you from the true reality of the situation.

Your karma with them blinds you from seeing their innocence. The motives blind you from seeing that they are all just trying to survive in a situation where their survival is not being threatened.

The Hidden Motives To Survive are distracting you from having a quiet mind and living an epic life. They are fraying your energy and pulling you in directions other than what you are committed to.

As a recap, here are the ten Hidden Motives To Survive creating fear, doubt, frustration, and uncertainty where there can easily be curiosity, joy, creativity, and inspiration.

1. **Pride** - Often experienced as arrogance. Trying to be more important and prove you are above others. Overly attached to being right about things. Trying to look smarter than others. The quality of having an excessively high opinion of oneself or one's importance.

2. **Greed** - The fear that there won't be enough opportunity, time, money, food, or resources. The intense and selfish desire for something for fear of not having enough.

3. **Victim** - Feeling powerless as if life is out of your control.

4. **Illogical Rules** - Unconsciously following rules that degrade you. Believing that these rules are appropriate, important, or valuable even though, with examination, they aren't real and they make your life worse.

5. **Humble** - Having or showing a modest or low estimate of one's own importance. Making yourself less than.

6. **Traitor** - Hiding your true feelings or thoughts for fear of losing a benefit.

7. **Lazy** - Avoiding hard things in an effort to keep a benefit. Avoiding activity or exertion: not energetic or vigorous.

8. **Resistance** – Pushing against ideas, activities, and people in an effort to protect against the loss of a benefit. The fear of a negative future.

9. **Hatred** – Intense dislike or ill will. Fear of differences. Broken expectations that turn into anger.

10. **Grudge** – Holding onto a persistent feeling of ill will or resentment to make sure bad things won't happen.

Diffusing the Hidden Motives To Survive is HOW you transcend the survival mind. Meaning, when you diffuse, reduce and ultimately eliminate the Hidden Motives To Survive that cause The Drunk Monkey to talk, you transcend the survival mind and experience a quiet mind. That's the ball game!

Can you see that when you remove Greed or Hatred from your consciousness, you are you literally removing the cause behind the effect called The Drunk Monkey?

You need a teacher to help you see the motives, and you need a healer to help you heal the imbalances in your consciousness.

That's me.

That's why understanding the nature of The Drunk Monkey, and what fuels its endless commentary, along with distinguishing The Hidden Motives To Survive is essential on your path to a quiet mind.

Are you ready? Let's go.

Chapter 19
Pride

The Google dictionary defines being proud as "the quality of having an excessively high opinion of oneself or one's importance."

Pride is a useful survival tactic. By making yourself more important, you have a strategy for manipulating the people around into giving you priority. Having priority is a strategic advantage that has been leveraged throughout millennia by the survival mind.

At the heart of this Hidden Motive To Survive is the fear of not being valued. Look around and you will see that being important to the other people is a survival strategy used by the masses.

When pride is present, you want to be right. You want to show your dominance. You want to be celebrated. Unfortunately, this automatically puts you at odds with others. Pride is a form of force, and when you exert it, you will experience an equal and opposite counter-force pushing against you, even in subtle ways.

When pride is present, you try to make yourself special. You are in competition with others. You are at odds with others. You try to be right. You make others wrong. You are forceful. You are arrogant. You are pushy.

All of these ways of being put you into fight or flight, the domain of The Drunk Monkey.

When you have pride about your religion, you exclude others, and you live in the illusion that we are separate. You are robbed of your peace by the ridiculous idea that God loves some people and not others.

Many of my students come to me limited by the Pride they have for their personal development techniques. They can't figure out why they are always in conflict with others. Yet, they consistently make other people wrong for not studying personal development. They torment their family, friends, and workmates with snooty arrogance about how smart they are for developing themselves. They don't realize Pride is repelling and in their desire to "uplift" others, they are actually pushing them away.

Parents often tap into Pride about how they raise their children or illogically believe that their child's perceived success implies they are a success too. Pride drives us to Follow Rules That Don't Exist and to have Opinions On Everything.

Are you seeing how the Hidden Motives To Survive fuel the Unconscious Reflexes of The Drunk Monkey?

Here are a series of statements, perspectives and points of view that indicate Pride is present in your experience.

- Sticking up for your beliefs without concern for other beliefs or perspectives

- Pride about putting your children's needs above your own

- "My way is the right way and there's nothing you are going to say to convince me otherwise"

- "I take pride in doing what you are supposed to do because that's what good people do"

- "I want to prove that I am valuable and I need to be acknowledged as valuable"

- "I don't want to be fat! I want to look good, damn it!!"

- Doing hard things to look like you are strong or important or smart

- Not backing down on issues

- Need to be important, popular or needed

- "I can degrade myself if I want to"

Having the awareness to see when Pride is active is essential for disarming this Hidden Motive To Survive.

Find the release meditations for the Hidden Motives To Survive here at matthewferry.com/motives

Chapter 20
Greed

Greed is the fear that there won't be enough. It manifests as an intense and selfish desire for something. Greed is based in lack.

Like the other Hidden Motives To Survive, Greed is deeply embedded in our consciousness.

As a person who has done a lot of inner work, you might be repulsed by the idea of Greed. "Matthew, I am intentionally generous and try to make a contribution everywhere I go." And while that is the opposite of Greed, the invisible energy field of Greed still exists within your consciousness.

In fact, I guarantee you that Greed influences you whether you know it or not. It's that pervasive within the survival mind.

Most people believe that Greed is related to money. Not true. Money is just the most obvious representation.

Greed also affects our relationships. Early on in life, we are blinded by the illusion that there is not enough love to be given out by our parents. Suddenly we are in a rivalry with our siblings. We are fighting for our parent's attention and love, but this is an illusion. Our parents do the best they can based on their fears, doubts, goals, and objectives to give us what we need to grow up and be self-sufficient.

Greed drives us to act ineffectively with our friends. We want their appreciation and approval. When they don't give it to us the way we want it, we become selfish or needy or resentful or angry or hold a grudge. Our Greed creates the very thing we are trying to avoid.

Greed drives us to overeat. To indulge. To hoard food.

Greed drives us to seek pleasure for fear that there won't be enough. For example, many people find that they feel greedy for more sex.

The fear that there won't be enough pleasure can manifest in overindulgence in sugar, alcohol, caffeine, drugs, TV, binge-watching shows, video games, shopping, and the gamut of internet-based distractions.

By now, you are beginning to see how the fear that there won't be enough is persuasive. You are beginning to see how Greed can get The Drunk Monkey talking.

Here are a series of statements, perspectives and points of view that indicate Greed is fueling The Drunk Monkey.

- Grab it while you can even if you don't need it
- Fear that there's not enough X (love, time, resources) to go around
- Intense desire for more food than is needed
- Intense desire for more money than is needed
- Intense desire for more sex than is needed

- Intense desire for more validation than is needed
- Hoard or hang onto what you have
- Accumulate more than you need and keep it from others
- Fear that someone will take what you have
- Fear that there won't be enough money

With awareness comes the opportunity to create a new context in the areas of your life where Greed is present. With reflection, you can spot it and use your skills to Recontextualize to get the mind to quiet down.

I also recommend that you listen to the release meditation for Greed as a strategy to remove its influence from your life.

Find the release meditations for all 10 Hidden Motives To Survive here at matthewferry.com/motives

Chapter 21
Victim

Human beings are pack animals. The majority of our behaviors are programs designed to help us survive in the group. Victim is a role that gets developed in your childhood. Being weak, needing help, pretending you can't do things are great ways to get your mom and dad to pay attention to you.

Being a Victim is a very useful way to manipulate the people around you. It works really well. When you are playing the Victim, you get people to feel sorry for you. Because human beings are naturally compelled to help the weak, when you demonstrate you are weak, you get all kinds of payoffs from the people around you.

Ultimately, being a Victim is a block to your full enlightenment. It's a block to personal power and control over your experience of life.

As a seeker of Quiet Mind Epic Life, you want it all. You want to feel empowered. You want to experience peace and joy.

But you get distracted. The Drunk Monkey and its underlying motives pull your attention away from what you want to focus on.

This can lead to moments of feeling defeated. Sometimes, the people you have to deal with and the tasks of your life can feel overwhelming.

If you are being honest with yourself, there are times when you feel like you have to push hard to make things happen. It can feel a little like life is against you. You know this feeling, right?

It creates highs and lows in your experience. Energy highs and lows. Emotional highs and lows. Productivity highs and lows.

The low moments cause you to overcompensate, or worse, compromise on what you really want. It's in those moments that you feel like you may never get the epic life you desire.

This is The Hidden Motive To Survive called Victim in action. When this motive is present in your awareness, you feel powerless; life is out of your control.

To counteract this feeling of being powerless or not in control, you might get apathetic and stop going after what you want. Then you don't get what you want and you feel even more victimized. It's a vicious cycle.

As a high-conscious person, feeling like a victim is actually offensive. It's repulsive in others and worse when you catch yourself playing the victim. Yet, it happens more than any of us want to admit.

Unfortunately, Victim is programmed into your point-of-view and behaviors. When Victim is present in your consciousness, it can be very subtle. It will take tremendous discernment for you to spot it.

Here are the tell-tale signs that Victim is activated in your consciousness.

- I'm not good enough
- I don't fit in
- I'm a disappointment
- I can't have what I want
- I wish life was different
- I'm not in control
- I don't want to deal with life - just leave me alone
- Life is hard
- I just want to be taken care of
- Other people have it easier than me

When you understand the motive to play the Victim, then you can have compassion for yourself. As a result, you will be able to consciously choose something else. By recognizing that Victim is not a bad thing, that it has been an important survival strategy, you are able to put it in an effective context.

I recommend that you listen to the release meditation for Victim as a strategy to remove its influence from your life.

Find the release meditations for all 10 Hidden Motives To Survive here at matthewferry.com/motives

Chapter 22
Illogical Rules

You want to achieve Quiet Mind Epic Life, and then you turn around and make another person wrong for not doing something right. Bam!

There goes your quiet mind, as you sink into the energy of against, wrong, have to, need to, should, and must. Rather than having peace, you experience the negativity of arrogance. One second you are flowing, and the next moment you are caught up in superiority, egotism, and pushing against something or someone.

This happens when you are being affected by the Hidden Motive To Survive called Illogical Rules.

Illogical Rules are old, outdated perspectives about how to live and behave appropriately. They seem perfectly logical to you because everyone you know follows them. They seem appropriate, important, and valuable. I'm sure at one time in the history of humanity they made sense. But today they don't make sense, but you keep following them like they do.

With intense awareness, the rules you follow to effectively or appropriately live your life are revealed to be untrue. They have just been myths this whole time. They are illogical because they make your life worse, but you defend them like they make your life better.

Illogical Rules tend to contain words that imply obligation and advice like "have to, need to, must, should, and shouldn't". By using these words, they sound real and valid. But with close examination, they are not real, and they rob you of your quiet mind by creating opposition in your world.

Illogical Rules cause you to feel disrupted. They don't have any real consequence in the world, but for some unconscious reason, they feel very important.

Here's a short list of Illogical Rules I've encountered in people on my journey so far.

- Put your children's needs above your own
- Family first/family is the most important thing
- A woman's job is to raise children
- You have to look your best for company
- You never leave your spouse
- Better to look good then be happy
- Keep your business private
- Be kind to visitors/strangers even though it's uncomfortable and you don't want to
- You have to take care of the people you grew up with
- God will punish you if you don't follow his laws

When you are ready to address the impact this Hidden Motive has on your path to a quiet mind, I suggest you listen to the release meditation found at this link: matthewferry.com/motives

Chapter 23
Humble

You want to be enlightened, but how could you possibly be enlightened? Isn't enlightenment reserved for the blessed, the revered, the saints, the gurus, the chosen few?

Now you have a conflict. You are driven to create a quiet mind. You know in your heart that it is the ultimate pursuit. You are voting with your time. You are all in. Yet, there is this doubt. There is a nagging feeling that perhaps having a quiet mind isn't in the cards for you.

The Drunk Monkey says things like, "Come on! Who the hell do you think you are? You are just a normal person living a normal life. Enlightened people are special. You're not special. You're not destined to be special."

Or worse, it says things like, "Your ego is so out of control that you really think you are going to be enlightened? Stop being so arrogant."

These are telltale signs the Hidden Motive To Survive call Humble is fueling The Drunk Monkey. As a result, you hold yourself back. You don't own who you are. You don't say, "I'm committed to being enlightened. I'm committed to being in a oneness state with everything."

Humble is a valuable survival strategy passed down from your ancestors when they were actually in survival mode. In the past, it was just practical to make sure they didn't upset the Alpha for fear of retaliation. Being humble was a very important strategy. It helped keep them alive. Today it is keeping you from living a fully enlightened life.

Being humble means having or showing a modest or low estimate of one's own importance. While this makes total sense when you are living via the law of the jungle, Humble will rob you of your quiet mind and limit your epic life in today's modern society.

Here are some statements, perspectives, and points of view that indicate Humble is driving The Drunk Monkey. See if you can relate:

- I am less than, but somehow won favor by being obedient or doing it right
- I don't want to offend God so I make myself less than
- I don't deserve to be happy
- Other people are better than me
- I'm nothing
- I don't need to be important
- I don't want to be pushy so I will take less than my share
- God will be offended if I show my true power
- The people around me will be agitated if I speak up

- What I think is not as important is what other people think

Today, I am giving you permission to rise up. Be exactly who you are. Don't allow Humble to diminish your perfection in any way.

Get your hands on the Humble Release Meditation at this link: matthewferry.com/motives

Chapter 24
Traitor

The Google dictionary defines Traitor as a person who betrays a friend, country or principle.

When the Hidden Motive To Survive called Traitor is present you feel like you need to hide how you really feel because it's too disruptive to the people around you.

In a subtle way, you aren't being truthful. That's the essence of being a Traitor.

This gets you into trouble because hiding yourself and your true power causes The Drunk Monkey to spend time defending your positions to an imaginary group of people in your head that you are having an argument with.

When you are being influenced by Traitor you hide your feelings or thoughts for fear of losing an imaginary benefit. You find yourself betraying your family, friends, and business associates by cloaking yourself for fear of not being accepted. You pretend to agree with the group when you really don't. You act like you are in survival when you are striving to thrive.

Think about how important this survival strategy has been in our evolution as a species. In the most basic survival situations, like a small family group trying to live off of the land, a free-thinking person would be punished, chastised, and even cast out for breaking the family protocols.

For many people today, it's still dangerous to be who you are. If one of your parents or a spouse is a low-conscious violent person, they could physically harm you for saying what you think. If you have a tyrannical boss, you could be publicly humiliated for saying what you think or even fired.

Being a Traitor is a really, really valuable survival skill. It's no wonder it is so present in the consciousness of all of mankind.

When your consciousness is being impacted by Traitor, you inaccurately believe, "I can't be who I really am and get what I want."

However, the truth is the exact opposite. You must be who you really are to get what you really want.

In other words, you get what you focus on.

From an Enlightened Perspective, you are whole, complete, and perfect exactly as you are. Your presence is a gift to the whole of mankind. To not be who you really are is degrading.

Here are some statements, perspectives, and points of view that indicate Traitor is driving The Drunk Monkey. See if you can relate:

- If I am my authentic self, there will be a negative consequence.

- I have an underlying agenda that I'm not being honest about.

- If I tell people what I really think, they will reject me or it might hurt their feelings.

- I have to pretend that I'm okay with all of this, but I'm really not.

- I don't want this life that I'm living, but I have to grit my teeth, smile and pretend I like it.

- I am pretending to be helpful to you, but I really have an agenda that is helpful to me.

- I know I'm right, but I'm going to pretend like I have am open to other points of view.

- I feel weak so I have to put on a show like I'm strong.

- I don't really love the person I'm with, but I don't want to deal with the consequence.

Today I want you to be honest with yourself. You are not at risk. You don't need the people in your life to understand you. You are not in a survival situation. Set your intention to release Traitor today.

Get the Traitor Release Meditation here: matthewferry.com/motives

Chapter 25
Lazy

When your consciousness is imbalanced by the Hidden Motive To Survive called Lazy, you no longer see life as easy, effortless, and enjoyable.

Lazy causes you to resist taking action. When Lazy is imbalanced, life feels hard. You just want to do nothing in response to whatever is happening.

Have you ever found yourself putting off the important tasks of your life? Procrastinating for no reason? You know the feeling. The Drunk Monkey just says, "I don't want to."

Rather than move your initiatives along in a positive and productive way, you surf the web.

Rather than have that tough conversation, you do mindless cleaning.

Rather than finish that project, you binge watch a show you have already seen.

You eat and eat and eat for no reason. You're not hungry, but you distract yourself by mindlessly sticking food in your mouth.

This is an imbalance. It's a survival strategy.

When you are in your enlightened state, when your mind is quiet and your life is epic, you want more. You don't want to avoid or run away.

When the Lazy imbalance is present, you avoid hard things in an effort to keep a benefit. You avoid excessive activity. You avoid exertion. You are not energetic. You are not vigorous. You feel unmotivated and uninspired, and you can't muster the inner strength to address life's challenges.

When Lazy is imbalanced, The Drunk Monkey convinces you to seek pleasure instead of doing what it takes to change your circumstances.

The Lazy imbalance makes you feel like pleasure is scarce. Therefore, you need to indulge yourself now and do the hard stuff later.

This is the opposite of how you feel in your Quiet Mind Epic Life state. In that state, you see abundance everywhere in your life. Your perspective energizes and uplifts you. There is no fear of doing hard things. There is no fear of losing out on the potential for pleasure now.

Lazy causes you to do what is easy and pleasurable and to avoid the pain of doing what is assumed to be hard. You will find your-self overindulging.

You know Lazy is imbalanced because you are overeating, and you may even be drawn to drugs and alcohol. You are trying to change your state because you aren't willing to feel what you are feeling.

When you feel overwhelmed, Lazy is often the cause. Suddenly you want to stop everything hard and just unplug. You will be drawn to procrastinate and seek simple and often destructive pleasures. When Lazy is imbalanced, The Drunk Monkey says, "I don't want to do that. It's going to be too much work. Let's watch videos instead."

Check out these telltale signs the Hidden Motive To Survive Lazy has activated the survival mind:

- My life is in God's hands
- If I have a man in my life, then I don't have to be a powerful, capable woman
- Why do I have to do this, I don't want to
- How come it can't be easy / I just want it to be easy
- Just go with the program and don't make any waves
- Why work hard when I can manipulate others to get what I want
- Just go with the flow, it will all work itself out in the end
- It's easier to hate you then to leave you
- Doing things half ass. Not finishing with integrity
- I don't want to do the work... I just want the results

Some of my clients also get confronted by "Anti-Lazy" perspectives and points of view. Here are a few that you may relate to:

- If it's not hard, then it's not worth it
- Hatred of lazy people almost like traitors they will ruin your plans and put you at risk
- You must work tirelessly and push through no matter what.

Whether you are dealing with Lazy or Anti-Lazy, you can reduce the impact of this Hidden Motive on your life.

Get the Lazy Release Meditation atmatthewferry.com/motives

Chapter 26
Resistance

When the Hidden Motive Resistance is imbalanced in your consciousness, you are either hesitant or pushing against your life because you fear a negative future. The Drunk Monkey puts you into a protective state.

When The Hidden Motive Resistance is activated you aren't able to step back and see the perfection of all that is.

Instead, you are present to what is wrong or what isn't working. You are experiencing a subtle fear that something is wrong, or something is going to be wrong. Quiet mind slips out of your reach.

With reflection, you see that Resistance is a positive survival state that helps you to move forward with caution. It has developed in consciousness over millennia and is still affecting you today.

Of course, the problem with that is that your life isn't bad, wrong, or dangerous. That's why it's so valuable to see this Hidden Motive in action.

You are focused on creating a quiet mind. You can't be interested in that unless your life is already safe and stable.

In your quiet mind state, you begin to see that what you resist will persist and what you accept will transform. So resisting something or someone only keeps the degrading energy in place.

Resistance is subtle. You are often blind to it. With quiet mind, you can see "I'm resisting." The awareness makes you flexible. You see that the resistance is disturbing your peace. You let it go, and peace returns.

When Resistance is imbalanced, you don't have the conscious awareness to think, "I'm resisting!" Instead, you think, "This situation is wrong." The Drunk Monkey comes to the rescue with its Unconscious Reflexes. Your mind is now dominated by unwanted thoughts.

It's actually really easy to tell when Resistance is imbalanced. If you are not experiencing peace and flow, then you are resisting.

In Resistance, you relate to your circumstances like they are fixed. Instead of seeing that your experience of the world is inside of you, your views are distorted. You believe you are the effect of the world that is out there.

With a quiet mind, you realize that you don't actually experience the circumstances themselves. You experience your relationship to the circumstances. Your relationship is what you say about it, how you describe it, and your reaction to it.

When Resistance is imbalanced, you take a stand against things. You are resisting. The Drunk Monkey says, "That is bad, and I don't want it" "They shouldn't act that way" "I hate when that happens".

This is distinct from a quiet mind state where all is well and you are in harmony with all that is. With a quiet mind you fear nothing. Everything appears to be a part of the oneness. You see the innate innocence of life, and there is nothing to resist.

Let's be clear, seeing the innocence of life doesn't mean you act irresponsibly. In quiet mind, you don't intentionally harm yourself by putting yourself in harm's way. You don't hide your head in the sand.

On the contrary, you are very clear-minded. You are very responsible and proactive. You seek integrity and workability above all else.

With a quiet mind, it's clear that some things are destructive and other things are constructive. It's also clear that resisting only degrades you.

In day-to-day life, there are all kinds of things to resist. Here are some strategies The Drunk Monkey uses when the Hidden Motive To Survive Resistance has been activated.

- Resisting negativity in order to promote positivity
- Not following the rules
- Gossiping

- Complaining
- Doing what you want vs. doing what you said
- Back talking
- Being rude
- Heckling
- Taking cheap shots
- Politicking

You know what to do. Get the Release Resistance Meditation here: matthewferry.com/motives

Chapter 27
Hatred

When your mind is quiet, you are in a state of peace, flow, and joy. You feel a connection to everyone and everything. You see the beauty in everything. You see the perfection of opposites. It's evident that good needs bad and bad needs good and that neither is right or wrong. Neither is better or worse. You see that opinion and perspective are the sources of all negative experiences.

When you are imbalanced by the Hidden Motives To Survive your mind is cluttered with The Drunk Monkey and all of its positions, opinions, distractions, and disruptions. It can seriously hinder your potential to thrive.

Hatred is a particularly destructive imbalance. It's not psychology. It's energetic. It's pervasive within survival consciousness.

Hatred is an intense dislike for someone or something. It is ill will. Hatred is the fear of differences or the fear that those differences will bring harm. It is broken expectations that turn into anger.

Don't resist Hatred. Celebrate it and accept that it's been a been a very important part of our survival as a species. What you accept you can transform.

Hatred helps us to focus on our enemy so that we can anticipate their every move. Hatred helps us to rally the troops and galvanize our focus against our foes. Hatred bands people together to enact social change.

Unfortunately, as a high-conscious person, hatred causes us to be deeply imbalanced. It fires up The Drunk Monkey and fills your mind with scenarios of violence, retaliation, vengeance, and ploys to intentionally harm others. It's a survival strategy that will cause you to malfunction while you are seeking to experience enlightened prosperity.

In order to experience a pervasively quiet mind, you must transcend this Hidden Motive To Survive. One way is to practice being in a neutral state. Not for or against. Accepting and appreciating all that is. This doesn't mean that you don't have preferences about what you want. It simply means you are not deploying Hatred for or against something in order to accomplish your objectives.

Here are so examples of Hatred, even in the simplest form, that will disturb your quiet mind:

- Hatred (Ill will) of people believe something different then I believe

- Hatred (Ill will) is a tool for maintaining your position that you are right

- Hatred (Ill will) of rich people or poor people

- Hatred of negative people

- Hatred of people who oppose me
- Hatred of obligation
- Hatred of being inconvenienced
- Hatred of being lied to
- Hatred of having to be responsible for myself

Ready to release Hatred? Get the Release Meditation here at matthewferry.com/motives

Chapter 28
Grudge

When the Hidden Motive To Survive called Grudge is present, you have a persistent feeling of ill will or resentment towards others or situations. A grudge is a feeling of resistance you have against an imaginary negative future based on a previous negative event.

For example, you walk over, pet a dog, and then the dog bites you. Now you imagine that all dogs might bite. Instead of admitting you are irrationally fearful based on a one-time event, you make up stories about the things you don't like about dogs. You have a grudge about dogs based on your past experience.

It's the long-term strategy that has its foundation in Hatred. The Drunk Monkey believes that if you stay angry, then you won't be hurt again. Holding a grudge makes you vigilant and ensures you Avoid Making The Same Mistake Twice.

Grudges are held to protect yourself from your enemies. While your ancestors had actual enemies, you likely accidentally live in the illusion that someone or something is your enemy. Most often, people are just doing what they are doing, you resist them then declare enemy status.

Grudge becomes imbalanced because you are conditioned to hate by the people in your family or society. If you grow up with the people around you constantly saying derogatory things about a particular person, group, or race, then these perspectives are the status quo you are accustomed to.

Remember, The Drunk Monkey loves to maintain the status quo as a way to ensure you remain part of the pack.

As a matter of survival, differences are treated as threats. Facial features, skin color, speech patterns, beliefs, and mannerisms all activate Grudge and get The Drunk Monkey spewing judgments, opinions, and unexamined beliefs.

When Grudge is imbalanced in our consciousness, we don't seek to understand. We don't want to accept or forgive. We are driven by The Drunk Monkey to protect ourselves.

When Grudge is imbalanced, you believe that forgiving people means you are weak and condoning their behavior. The Drunk Monkey tells you that you would put yourself at risk of being affected by their behavior if you forgive them. Better to hate them, resist them, and hold the grudge.

From an Enlightened Perspective, you realize that all Grudges can be forgiven because they are just arbitrary positions that you have taken. You see that they are only hurting you. You realize that your opinions are just vanities.

With a quiet mind, all of Drunk Monkey insanity can be released in favor of peace, tranquility, and flow. It's effortless because you realize that opinions are inherently bogus. Opinions are the source of your suffering, and since you are devoted to Quiet

Mind Epic Life, you naturally release opinions that rob you of your peace.

Here are some ways to spot this Hidden Motive To Survive in action:

- Making up a story about someone and then being mad them for it
- Not liking someone else for the things they have because I don't have them
- Being jealous of others
- Holding something against someone without their knowledge
- I don't like the way you look
- I don't like that you do things differently the me
- I'm not going to forget the time you did something bad to me
- I will not forgive you
- Disliking others based on their race, gender or sexual orientation
- Thinking others have it easier than you do

Enlightenment is the recognition that the source of life within you is the source of life in everyone and everything else. We are all one thing expressing itself with infinite variety.

As a high-conscious person, there is no value in having ill will or resentment towards others or situations. It's simply not worth continuing to be influenced by the Hidden Motives To Survive while robbing yourself of experiencing a quiet mind.

Now is the time to release Grudge along with all the other Hidden Motives To Survive, so you can enjoy the benefits of living with enlightened prosperity.

You can find all the Hidden Motive Release Meditations here: matthewferry.com/motives

Chapter 29
Accepting Your New Awareness

To quiet the mind, you must make the decision that you are no longer interested in The Drunk Monkey and its motivations. The Drunk Monkey is a talking machine. It isn't interested in your peace. It doesn't really care about your intentions. It is an impersonal biological mechanism.

Transcending the mind and its motives will be one of the most profoundly beautiful experiences of your life. You might initially feel concerned that if you aren't thinking, then you won't be able to function. The exact opposite is true. When you aren't thinking automatically, you are able to deal with your life sensibly and with otherworldly power.

This is because, as your mind goes quiet, you begin to see things that other people can't see. It becomes very clear that The Drunk Monkey and all of its insanity have been blocking you from seeing the world as it is.

The drive to *stay* alive has blinded you from the beauty and grandeur of *being* alive.

In silence, a new reality begins to appear. You start to see that you live inside of an energetic ocean. You begin to notice that solidity and the notion that you can be separate from others (from God and from the world) are illusions.

Mystical abilities begin to develop. You can premeditate what will happen. Your presence heals people. What is imbalanced becomes balanced when you are involved. Your level of clarity, calm, and certainty seems extraordinary to the people around you.

I personally became fascinated with science. I found that modern atomic physics and theoretical physics made perfect sense to me. It explained in scientific terms what had been revealed to me when my mind went quiet.

I found answers within the scientific field of consciousness. I'm not a scientist, I'm a mystic. I enjoy studying science as a hobby. For me it was helpful, but for you, it might be uninteresting.

Over the years, I've found that there are entire bodies of peer-reviewed studies that demonstrate the existence of what was once thought of as mystical hocus-pocus.

I took solace in the recognition that extra-sensory perception was no longer a myth. Precognition, psychokinesis, distance healing, and distant viewing are now demonstrated in peer-reviewed experiments all over the world. The technology, intelligence, and curiosity of science have caught up with the intuitive conclusions of the mystics. Consciousness is no longer a theory - it's a real thing.

It turns out, thoughts are not in the brain. We are not separate beings. We are interconnected at the atomic level. Contained within the Zero Point Field Theory is proof that God exists.

Cells are affected by our thoughts. Genes turn on and off based on our perspectives about life. The placebo effect is scientifically documented to heal people.

It is very common for physicists to transform during their studies and start behaving in accordance to spiritual truths and doctrine. They don't change their behavior because they are religious. In fact, they are often agnostic. They change because science removes the ignorance of genetic, familial, and societal programming and reveals the profound inter-connectivity of the nature of the universe.

While Einstein was perplexed by what he called "spooky action at a distance", you likely experience it on a regular basis. Oftentimes you know who's calling before the phone rings. You don't know why you have answers to questions you don't know anything about. The answer just comes to you. People seem to feel better in your presence. You probably never considered that it's a form of healing. Maybe you have felt like your soul lifted out of your body. You might have had dreams where you see what will happen in your future. You could even have had experiences where you knew about a place that you had never been.

My friend, you are a mystic, and you just need to accept it. Embrace it because it's about to get way more intense. You are about to start seeing with more clarity than you have ever seen in your life.

I have found that it can be a little disruptive at first. If you look into a person's eyes and you see what ails them, it can throw you for a loop. If you walk into a room and you get overwhelmed with the feeling of victim and grief, it can knock you off balance.

First of all, you will get used to it.

Second of all, you will learn how to *use* it. Each of us has our own special gifts that get revealed when we achieve a quiet mind state.

Like I've said before, having a quiet mind gives you an unbelievable strategic advantage. The paradox is that you won't need the advantage because you will, maybe for the first time in your life, feel completely safe and secure within yourself. There will be nowhere to go, nothing to do, and nothing will be incomplete.

This is ultimate freedom.

The Daily Practices
Attaining & Maintaining a Quiet Mind

Are you ready for some daily practices that maintain your Quiet Mind Epic Life?

Following are 23 practices designed to ensure that the processes discussed in this book stay top of mind and get integrated into your real life.

As you embrace these practices, they will naturally make you aware of The Unconscious Reflexes of The Drunk Monkey and the underlying Hidden Motives To Survive.

That awareness is critical.

If your mind is in survival mode, then there is no peace for you. If you can't spot The Unconscious Reflexes of The Drunk Monkey and the Hidden Motives To Survive, then you will never be able to achieve a quiet mind. If you can't spot yourself being influenced by the Hidden Motives like greed or victim, then you will never be able to keep your mind quiet.

The more you use these practices, the more aware you will become.

Remember that awareness makes you flexible, which reveals new options. These new options are the basis of increased power. Furthermore, when you have options, you feel empowered and safe, which releases your mind's motive to think.

The 23 Daily Practices are Recontextualizations. They will help you develop the skill of describing the conditions and circumstances in a way that creates an empowering reality for you.

Remember that "Life ain't nothin' 'til you call it." If you are going to make things up, you might as well make things up that feel good and give you power. These practices help you do that.

When something is off in your life, your mind is triggered into survival mode and you are bombarded with unwanted thoughts. To get the mind to quiet down, you must restore your integrity.

Remember, restoring integrity doesn't mean having better morals and values. Integrity means being functional, workable, whole, and complete. Restoring your integrity means restoring workability in your life with quality thoughts and activities.

To create Quiet Mind Epic Life, you must push yourself to restore your personal integrity. When you do, you will notice yourself taking responsibility rather than blaming someone else. You will practice healthy communication, rather than hiding your true feelings. You will also notice yourself canceling agreements that were made out of guilt and obligation.

My recommendation is that you take one of these 23 practices on per day. Simply read the description in the morning, and then diligently put it into practice in your life.

I want you to experience Quiet Mind Epic Life!

Day 1 Practice
Set your intention to be happy regardless of the circumstance.

To develop a Quiet Mind Epic life, practice setting the intention to be happy regardless of the circumstances.

Just say it now, "Please set the intention to be happy regardless of my circumstances today."

Rather than being at the effect of The Drunk Monkey and its barrage of foolish imaginations, take conscious control of your mental state. Rehearse being happy regardless of the circumstances in your mind throughout the day. See the day ahead and see yourself being happy no matter what happens.

Today, release all your conditions for happiness. The stuff like, "If my spouse does X then I will be happy." Give up your conditions!

If I get the money that I want, then I will be happy.

If my son cleans his room, then I will be happy.

If I get on the scale and I've lost weight, then I will be happy.

If my mom doesn't become a blubbering idiot at dinner tonight, then I will be happy.

Name one of your If/Then's for happiness right now. Just say it to yourself.

Be honest with yourself.

Now just admit that you are being an ignorant low conscious fool. Be honest. Happiness is a matter of context. Nothing outside of you in the world makes you happy. No one needs to do anything for you to be happy. Happiness is the recognition that all is well.

Remember the Quiet Mind Epic Life Recontextualization statements that produce Enlightened Perspectives?

- You choose to come to Earth.
- You keep coming back.
- You choose the general circumstances.
- You thought this general configuration of life would make for some interesting experiences.
- Your soul is happy about both positive and negative experiences. They have equal value.

Happiness and peace are not conditional. The conditions are just stories The Drunk Monkey tells you. The Drunk Monkey is trying to protect you from experiencing negativity and getting positive benefits. But you have no idea what will happen today. It's all just your best guess.

Set your intention to be happy regardless of the circumstances. Remember that an Enlightened Perspective is always there, available, and ready to transform your experience.

As you embrace Enlightened Perspectives, you get to choose your experience of life. You are no longer at the effect of life. That is real freedom. That is what creates Quiet Mind Epic Life.

Day 1 Enlightened Perspectives

- I choose to come to Earth.
- I keep coming back.
- I choose the general circumstances.
- I thought this general configuration of life would make for some interesting experiences.
- My soul is happy about both positive and negative experiences. They have equal value.

Day 2 Practice
Practice total and complete acceptance

Practice total and complete acceptance of all people in all situations at all times including yourself is critical for developing a quiet mind. To accept is also to be non-resistant. The Hidden Motive Resistance causes The Drunk Monkey to engage and start cluttering up your mind.

Try this. Admit that you have no idea who you are, who other people are, what's happening in the world and that you are just making things up. Try that perspective on all day and notice the amazing result.

The Drunk Monkey is a distinguishing machine. It's on the lookout for differences. It wants to identify anything potentially harmful. When people don't act the way you think they should, The Drunk Monkey starts judging and strategizing how to deal with the threat.

Stop protecting yourself from people who aren't attacking. Be honest today. Your life is almost completely safe. The people in your life are doing the best they can. Behaving differently than you, doesn't make them wrong or bad or dangerous or a threat.

Today just admit that you are not the ruler of the universe. Admit that no one signed up for your perfect behavior plan. No one is asking you how they should behave. The Drunk Monkey is arrogant because it is ignorant.

Just keep saying to yourself, "People are doing the best they can given their perspective. My opinion that they should be different is the source of my suffering."

Really push yourself to honor the perfection of all the imperfection. Really notice the beauty in all people, especially those people you normally disagree with.

Practice seeing things from their perspective. Practice seeking to understand why they do what they do.

Accept people exactly as they are - but don't tolerate being harmed or degraded. You can accept the existence the black widow spider without resisting it but that doesn't mean you sleep with it in your bed.

Honor where people are coming from but don't allow yourself to be degraded because of it. Understand people's perspective, but that doesn't mean you have to like it. You can have a preference and remain peaceful at the same time.

All of that applies to you as well. Practice accepting yourself exactly as you are. Really seek to understand why you are the way you are. Acknowledge your motives for thinking, believing and behaving. Accept that, until now, you were doing the best you could.

Celebrate the empowerment of being able to see yourself with discerning, non-judgmental eyes for perhaps the first time in your life. What a victory.

As you embrace Enlightened Perspectives, you get to choose your experience of life. You are no longer at the effect of life. That is real freedom. That is what creates Quiet Mind Epic Life.

Day 2 Enlightened Perspectives

- I am a soul.

- The soul is infinite.

- We are all one thing expressing itself with an infinite variety.

- There is no one out there, just my interpretations.

Day 3 Practice
Acknowledge and appreciate the people in your life.

You will naturally achieve Quiet Mind Epic Life when you practice acknowledging and appreciating the people in your life. Especially the people who normally bother you. When you are bothered, your mind is disturbed and quiet mind is not possible.

The Drunk Monkey is hyper-focused on what's wrong with people. It is constantly judging them. It is barraging you with commentary and opinions about other people. If you haven't noticed, you can't count on The Drunk Monkey to say anything nice.

The Drunk Monkey is trying to prove that it is worthy of other people's love. It is constantly rationalizing your behavior in comparison to others. It will try to prove that you are a victim and you deserve sympathy. It will waste your time playing out scenarios to prove that you are better than other people.

All that mind chatter goes quiet when you practice acknowledging and appreciating people. In essence, you are telling The Drunk Monkey, all is well. My place in the tribe is secure. There is no need to jostle for position with all your strategizing and posturing.

Today intentionally practice appreciating...

- How people look

- How they operate

- What they do

- Their smallest positive qualities and characteristics

While you are at it, appreciate yourself. How you look, operate and what you do. All is well. You are whole, complete and perfect.

As you embrace Enlightened Perspectives, you get to choose your experience of life. You are no longer at the effect of life. That is real freedom. That is what creates Quiet Mind Epic Life.

Day 3 Enlightened Perspectives

- Everyone I know and every I see is an infinite being.

- We are all expressions of the same energy and information.

- I do not like in other people what I'm unwilling to admit about myself.

Day 4 Practice
Stop holding people accountable to agreements they never made.

You can't hold people accountable to agreements that they didn't make and still have a quiet mind. The contrast and uncertainty of people not doing what you expect them to do is a natural trigger for The Drunk Monkey to invade your mindshare and rob you of your peace.

Today just recognize that no one signed up to follow your rules. Your rules about life are not the right ones. No one actually cares about what you think.

The Drunk Monkey is doing its best to navigate being a human. It is following rules that are the result of genetic programs. It follows rules based on karma which is just old outdated information from your soul. It was programmed to believe the way your family and culture did things was the right way of living.

Open yourself up to all the possibilities of the moment. You have no idea how good it's going to get. The Drunk Monkey premeditates bad stuff. Take back control and premeditate good stuff. Trust that all is well. Trust that it's always going your way, even when it's not.

You have no idea how anything is "supposed to be." You are doing your best to get life to turn out the way you want. Sometimes you need to surrender to what's happening around you. People are doing the best they can. Give them some grace today. Stop holding them accountable to rules they didn't agree to.

As you embrace Enlightened Perspectives, you get to choose your experience of life. You are no longer at the effect of life. That is real freedom. That is what creates Quiet Mind Epic Life.

Day 4 Enlightened Perspectives

- No one signed up for my accountability program.
- Incarnating as a human on Earth is like my soul taking a vacation from being infinite.
- I choose to incarnate with the people in my life.
- I choose the major negative experiences of my life before incarnating on Earth.

Day 5 Practice
Use appreciation.

If you have someone who isn't behaving the way you want, use appreciation to change their behavior.

If you try to force them to change, they will resist. If you try to manipulate them, they will resist. What you resist will persist What you accept and therefore appreciate, will transform.

I'm just going to keep going after this idea of appreciation because it is so transformational.

A quiet mind is a result of the recognition that we are all one thing expressing itself with infinite variety.

Therefore, there is nothing to fear or be concerned about.

Here's the bottom line, no fear and no mind chatter.

Mind chatter is an expression of your survival mind.

An enlightened mind, is a quiet mind.

A quiet mind is a powerful mind.

A quiet mind is influential because it has transcended fear and resistance.

When you transcend the survival mind and you connect with your infinite nature, you naturally experience love, appreciation and respect for all things and all people.

When fear is present, the survival mind is creating the illusion that you are at risk. You can't see people for who they really are when you are trying to survive.

You get what you give.

The people around you are a mirror of what you are putting out into the world.

If you use force, then you will be met with force. When you are met with force you engage fight or flight. That means your creativity, resourcefulness and your joy evaporate.

Let's do some recontextualization together.

You are not the behavior police.

Your resistance is just your ignorance.

The Drunk Monkey is misrepresenting someone else's behavior as a threat. See the illusion that you are separate. See the illusion that you are not getting what you want.

Appreciate people exactly as they are, their differences are not bad and their differences are not a threat.

Admit that you are making the situation bad with your resistance.

The other people are just doing what they are doing. If you would prefer to have people behave differently, lead with appreciation.

Appreciate their perspective, appreciate their motivations and seek to understand. Be curious rather than judgemental.

When you resist people, they naturally resist you. Resistance is a very destructive habit. It takes your energy. It takes your happiness. It takes your momentum.

It robs you of your quiet mind.

When you resist others, you are causing yourself to suffer and then you are blaming them.

Please stop pretending that other people are affecting your happiness. Only your perspective and your preferences are affecting your happiness. They are in a no-win situation.

They can't be themselves around you. You are repressing them with your judgments. You lose. They lose.

People are doing the best they can at the moment given their perspective on life.

If you have someone who isn't behaving the way you want, use appreciation to change their behavior.

I have found that sometimes you have to give up your resistance first.

Start by admitting that you are not the ruler of the universe. Then admit that people are doing the best they can based on their environment, conditioning, and perspective.

Mentally make a list of everything you appreciate about them. Then fantasize about the new behaviors you want to see them doing.

Then do the most powerful thing of all: Acknowledge and appreciate them!!!

Here's the crazy thing...

They already do many, many, things that please you but you have been blind to it.

When you see something that you like, acknowledge them.

Say it out loud!!

If you have someone who isn't behaving the way you want, use appreciation to change their behavior.

This will deactivate the survival mind and create a quiet mind.

When your mind goes quiet you will be introduced to a new reality,

Imagine feeling completely free, completely at home, completely safe and completely at ease.

Oooooooooo.... It feeeeeels soooooo gooood.

Take a deep breath in with me right now, hold it as long as you can, and set your intention with me.

Please set the intention to use appreciation to change people's behavior.

Please set the intention to release force, manipulation, and resistance to change people's behavior.

Please set the intention to accept people exactly as they are.

Remember, The Enlightened Perspective is always there, it's always ready to transform your experience from resistance to peace, from uncertainty to profound trust and knowing that all is well.

Enlightenment is the recognition that the source of life within you is the source of life in everyone and everything else.

We are all one thing, expressing itself with infinite variety.

As you embrace Enlightened Perspective, you get to choose your experience of life.

You are no longer at the effect of life and That is real freedom.

That is what creates a Quiet Mind Epic Life.

Please set the intention to use appreciation to change people's behavior.

Keep me in the loop. I want to know what you are experiencing.

We are in this together.

As you embrace Enlightened Perspectives, you get to choose your experience of life. You are no longer at the effect of life. That is real freedom. That is what creates Quiet Mind Epic Life.

Day 5 Enlightened Perspectives

- I am not in charge.
- No one signed up for my life plan.
- We are all infinite beings
- You are not the behavior police.
- Your resistance is just your ignorance.

Day 6 Practice
Be kind to people even when they don't operate the way you think they should.

Kindness will release your resistance; which will quiet your mind and set you up for an epic life.

Just admit that you have a preference about how people should operate. Start there. Be honest. You want people to do what you want them to do. It's okay, we all do.

The problem is that your preference gets misrepresented by The Drunk Monkey as a "must" or you are uncomfortable. Discomfort gets your mind talking and disturbs your peace. Discomfort is a perspective and therefore it's a choice.

Let's dig deeper. Your preference doesn't mean you are right. For example, liking chocolate doesn't make vanilla bad.

Today notice that The Drunk Monkey generalizes and makes people who like vanilla wrong and dangerous. The Drunk Monkey resists difference.

Be honest. Being upset with people who like vanilla is literally stupid. You being upset with people who don't operate the way you think is equally stupid.

313

They are not actually a threat to you. The Drunk Monkey has decided that people who behave the way you expect them to are right and people who don't are wrong.

Resisting them robs you of your peace. They are not robbing you of your peace. It's The Drunk Monkey's fantasy that they are a threat that is robbing you of your peace.

Accept them as they are. Appreciate that they see the world differently than you do. Push to recognize that they simply approach the world in a way that you might not understand.

Accept them but don't tolerate being treated poorly or in a way that degrades you. There is no benefit to resisting the black widow spider. There is also no benefit in interacting with it and putting yourself at risk.

Today just wake up. Open yourself up to all the differences out there. There is an infinite variety of people, behaviors, cultures and preferences. No one operates the same way you do.

Remember that you didn't decide to operate this way. Your preferences are mostly based on what you got used to in your environment. That doesn't make your preferences better. That just makes you an unconscious meat sack! Please give the other unconscious meat sacks some grace today, would you?

As you embrace Enlightened Perspectives, you get to choose your experience of life. You are no longer at the effect of life. That is real freedom. That is what creates Quiet Mind Epic Life.

Day 6 Enlightened Perspectives

- The world is perfect exactly as it is. The only thing that makes it imperfect is my perspective about it.

- The people in my life are perfect exactly as they are. The only thing that makes them imperfect is my perspective about them.

- I am not the ruler of the universe.

- No one actually cares about my perspective other than me. If someone aligns with my beliefs it's because of common interests not because it's the truth.

Day 7 Practice
Practice being unoffendable.

To accelerate your goal of experiencing Quiet Mind Epic Life, simply practice being "unoffendable."

When you are offended, you are in a defensive position which is the domain of The Drunk Monkey. When you engage The Drunk Monkey, you are disturbed and your peace is gone.

You are only offended because you are ignorant. Someone says, "Blah blah blah" and then you label it in a way that hurts your feelings. Are you nuts? Why would you do that? Take responsibility for your interpretations today.

Your friend says she will do one thing, then she does another. The Drunk Monkey screams, "Traitor!"

Your friend broke her word. But that doesn't make her bad. So, your expectations got broken. That happens to you thousands of times per year. There is no reason to arbitrarily decide her behavior is offensive this time. Use your skills of Recontextualization, and let her off the hook.

Be unoffendable today. For your sake. For your peace. Because you deserve to have an amazing life. Because a quiet mind leads you to an epic life.

As you embrace Enlightened Perspectives, you get to choose your experience of life. You are no longer at the effect of life. That is real freedom. That is what creates Quiet Mind Epic Life.

Day 7 Enlightened Perspectives

- Nothing offends me unless I assign a meaning that threatens my perspective.

- All things good, bad, right and wrong are the same thing.

- If I'm going to make things up, I might as well make up things that feel good and empower me.

- God is impersonal and does not care because it is the source of all things.

- God cannot be offended because there is no such thing as right and wrong.

- All actions, attitudes, and beliefs have consequences and there is no need for me to administer them.

Day 8 Practice
Make a contribution to everyone you meet.

Today I want you to make a contribution to everyone you meet at minimum by honoring and accepting who they are.

Quiet Mind Epic Life is an expression of non-resistance and non-attachment. You give up your opinions about how the world should be and devote yourself to honoring how the world appears to you. When you honor how the world appears to you, it transforms into something infinitely more beautiful and appealing.

Your relationship with others is one of the biggest sources of conflict and discomfort. When you are in conflict or uncomfortable, The Drunk Monkey dominates your mindshare and robs you of the peace that is rightfully yours.

Today make a concerted effort to embrace the people in your life with love and a desire to honor them exactly as they are.

Push yourself to make a contribution to the people you encounter today. Be kind.

Be curious about people. Honor them as they are. Accept them as they are. Focus on them. Look people in the eye. Be present.

This will take some effort.

The Drunk Monkey judges people based on arbitrary rules that don't exist and then dismisses them. If they don't look right, smell right, act right, or say the right things, The Drunk Monkey withdraws your attention. You go unconscious as a way of escaping the conversation.

The Drunk Monkey in your head is on autopilot. It assumes that people are irrelevant, and not helpful to you. It tells you to ignore people and move on quickly. "I've got no time for this person today," it says.

It assumes your life is short. Your time is short. You have no time. You are a victim of time. These are all invalid survival-based perspectives that have no basis in reality.

When your mind is quiet, there is no sense of time whatsoever.

At its worst, The Drunk Monkey assumes that the people you are encountering throughout your day might be potentially dangerous and therefore, it looks for differences in other people. As a matter of basic survival, it judges, assesses, analyzes, and makes up stories.

Today, let all that go. Honor each person's viewpoint. Accept people exactly as they are. Recognize they are doing the best they can. Tell The Drunk Monkey there is nothing to fear. Acknowledge that their point of view is not a threat to you, even if you disagree with it. Just appreciate their perspective.

Listen. Ask questions. Be curious. Seek to understand what they are committed to. Try to figure out what they are interested in and what they are working on in their life. Find out what is important to the people you encounter today.

Set your intention to make a contribution to them in some way. Remember that honoring and accepting people is one of the most valuable contributions you can make.

Today you will discover that when you focus on others, your mind starts to go quiet.

As you embrace Enlightened Perspectives, you get to choose your experience of life. You are no longer at the effect of life. That is real freedom. That is what creates Quiet Mind Epic Life.

Day 8 Enlightened Perspectives

- Honoring and accepting people as they are is the greatest contribution I can make to humanity.

- Enlightenment is the recognition that the source of life within me is the source of life in everyone and everything else.

- We are all one thing expressing itself with infinite variety.

- We are all one thing. Like a grove of trees. We all spawned from the same source. Just a variation on the theme.

Day 9 Practice
Solve problems by getting into alignment and then redirecting.

You will naturally achieve Quiet Mind Epic Life when you are in alignment with life and embracing it exactly as it is. Resisting your life in any way will cause The Drunk Monkey to engage and rob you of your peace.

Face your problems today. Accept that they are there. Don't resist. Trust that all is well.

Step back and recognize the only reason you are resisting the issues in your life is because Hidden Motives To Survive and Unconscious Reflexes have been activated. In other words, your perception and the way you are labeling the situation is causing your resistance. The issue is what it is.

Find alignment with your problems. Meaning, find a way to make them right. Find the definitions and the descriptions that bring you back to neutral.

Remember the three umpires story? "It ain't nothin' 'til you call it." You get to call it. You get to define it. If you are going to make things up, why not make things up that feel good and empower you?

To be in alignment creates integrity within you. You become fortified. You start to function better.

Resistance causes you to malfunction. You can't focus. You aren't creative. Problem-solving is so much easier when you have your faculties intact.

When you are in resistance you see life as fixed, permanent and unmovable. You see the world as if it is only one way and there are no options. When you feel like there are no options you turn yourself into a victim. This false perspective closes you off to the new ideas that are out of the box.

Einstein didn't solve mysteries of the universe by being resistant, stressed and frustrated. He didn't frantically go after the problems he was trying to solve. He released it. He opened himself up. He took naps. He went for bike rides.

Chill out! Being at peace makes you more creative. When your creativity is restored, ingenuity and inspiration start to take over and you discover your optimism.

Release your attachment to the outcome. The Drunk Monkey has exaggerated fears about losing positive benefits and experiencing negative results. It fantasizes. It dreams. It makes up stories. Bust The Drunk Monkey! Don't let it get away with exaggerating.

Challenge The Drunk Monkey by forcing it to look at the Worst Case Scenario. Then make plans to deal with the Worst Case Scenario (See Appendix A) should it come. Don't try to avoid the worst case. Play it out in your mind. Go all the way to the absolute worst thing that could happen. Show The Drunk Monkey that you have what it takes to deal with the bad things that come your way.

Then declare your problems and issues a blessing. A lesson. An exercise in growing. None of these things are any more or less true than the labels you are currently giving your problems.

As you embrace Enlightened Perspectives, you get to choose your experience of life. You are no longer at the effect of life. That is real freedom. That is what creates Quiet Mind Epic Life.

Day 9 Enlightened Perspectives

- Life isn't anything until I call it something.
- All is well.
- Destruction and creation are the same things just at different places in the timeline.
- Breakdown is the beginning of a breakthrough.

Day 10 Practice
It's always me, it's never them.

Your mind will go quiet and set you up for an epic life when you stop blaming other people for your experience. Blame is a form of protection, and it engages The Drunk Monkey to rob you of your peace.

Blaming others also robs you of your power. When you blame others you are connected to the Hidden Motive To Survive called Victim. It's a filter. It makes you feel out of control. It makes you feel like you are at the effect of life.

Release Victim right now. Just say it out loud. "Release Victim."

Today, take radical responsibility. Take responsibility for everything you are experiencing. You can't control the situation. But you can control your perspective about it. Your perspective determines how you feel. How you feel is how you respond.

If you point fingers at other people and blame them for you not feeling good, then you misrepresent reality. The reality is that no one makes you feel anything. They do something or say something. You label it. Your label gives you the experience.

Take radical responsibility for your experience of life. Not because it's true, but because it is empowering. Meaning you are not responsible for how life goes or what people do.

Take responsibility for your experience of the situation because it is empowering to you.

Complaining is selfish and destructive to you. When you complain you are weakening yourself. You inaccurately present a reality that implies you are limited. Complaining is just dumb. Stop that today.

Gossiping hurts you and is ignorant. In Chapter 8 I showed you that there are words, phrases, and concepts that cause your arm to go strong and others that make your arm go weak. Gossiping causes everyone's arm to go weak.

Gossiping is a feeble attempt at making yourself better than others by making them lower than you. Unfortunately, there are no other people out there in the world. Yes, there are people out there. But your experience of them is entirely in your head. You do not like in other people what you either A) won't admit about yourself, B) something you don't like about yourself or C) something you have worked to overcome.

It's never them, it's always you.

Getting upset is a waste of time. The Buddha said it like this, "Holding onto anger is like grasping a **hot coal** with the intent of throwing it at someone else; you are the one who gets burned."

People are doing the best they can given their perspective about life. They might create a physical or tangible effect on you, but they don't create an emotional effect. That's all you.

In the end, the only thing that annoys you about other people is your opinion. Opinions are the source of suffering.

As you embrace Enlightened Perspectives, you get to choose your experience of life. You are no longer at the effect of life. That is real freedom. That is what creates Quiet Mind Epic Life.

Day 10 Enlightened Perspectives

- It's always me. It's never them.

- People are doing the best they can.

- Negativity is the resistance I have to how life appears in my perception.

Day 11 Practice
Practice being in a state of appreciation.

Quiet Mind Epic Life springs forth from the realization that all is well, there is nothing to fear and my life is perfect exactly as it is. Resisting life in any way is foolish as it diminishes your creativity and resourcefulness and limits your ability to make effective changes.

Today be very intentional about seeing the good qualities of life. Push yourself to truly enjoy the good, the bad, and the ugly. You do this by focusing on Enlightened Perspectives. Which means you have a full understanding of the situation.

Notice the architecture. Be grateful for cars, buses, trains and planes. Really appreciate the role everyone plays in your life. Including all the people you might disagree with. Honor their perspective. Put yourself in their shoes and notice that, from where they stand, their behavior is correct. Appreciate that.

Appreciate yourself. Take stock of all the parts of your body that are functioning. Focus on how wonderful it is to have the faculties you have. Look at yourself in the mirror naked and find the part of your body that you appreciate and enjoy. Ignore the ones you have a judgment about. Just appreciate what is good, what is right, what is working and what you find attractive.

Appreciate the journey you've had so far. Take stock and notice how much you have learned and grown from all the things you called "bad" at the time.

Appreciate the idea that learning is really just failure done over and over until you can do it. Let go of anything you are still holding onto regarding your lack of results, your stupidity, or your failure. Forgive yourself. You are learning and growing.

Appreciate all the situations you are in today. Notice how much good there is in the world and in your world. You have so many advantages, tools, capabilities, allies, people, organizations, civil services, and other services at your disposal. You are living in the most opulent and abundant time in the history of mankind. Own it.

As you embrace Enlightened Perspectives, you get to choose your experience of life. You are no longer at the effect of life. That is real freedom. That is what creates Quiet Mind Epic Life.

Day 11 Enlightened Perspectives

- Acceptance and appreciation are some of the most powerful contributions I can make to humanity.

- We are all one thing expressing itself with infinite variety.

- Everything I see and experience is just an interpretation of the energy and information my five senses are picking up.

- Life isn't anything until I call it something.

Day 12 Practice
Find joy in every activity.

The more you embrace life in every way, the more Quiet Mind Epic Life you have.

Resistance is an expression of powerlessness and protection. If you resist, The Drunk Monkey talks, and you lose your peace of mind.

Today find joy in every activity no matter what it is. Joy is the natural result of knowing that all is well. When you have released the illusion that you are threatened or at a disadvantage, you will naturally take a deep breath and joy will rise.

Joy can be found in the present moment. Focus helps to create this state. Today focus on every activity you are doing with an intention of enjoying it.

Change your story today. Create a new context that serves you. Say something uplifting about every activity you do today. You get to choose. You can resist if you want, but that just seems dumb.

If you are disgruntled, are you optimal? Are you uplifted? Are you having fun? Are you joyful? NO! And who did that to you? You did it with your labels and descriptions. If you are going to make things up, why not make things up that feel good?

Today focus on your GEM's.

- G = Gratitude. Spend the day thinking about what you are grateful for. This will cause your mind to quiet down because there will be nothing for it to protect you against.

- E = Experience. You are here on Earth to experience. So what do you want to experience? You get to choose. Today keep setting your intention to enjoy your life.

- M = Manifestation. When you are grateful for what you have, enjoying the situation as it is, you become fertile ground for new wonderful things to start happening to you. As the inspiration strikes, focus on things you are manifesting or creating in your life.

Ask yourself these questions today.

- What do I enjoy about this?
- What am I learning from this?
- How can I get more enjoyment from this?

As you embrace Enlightened Perspectives, you get to choose your experience of life. You are no longer at the effect of life. That is real freedom. That is what creates Quiet Mind Epic Life.

Day 12 Enlightened Perspectives

- There is joy available to me at all times in all activities.

- People are perfect exactly as they are. All imperfection is the result of applying arbitrary standards and measurements that don't exist in reality.

- All is well.

- My life and all thing components of it are perfect exactly as they are.

Day 13 Practice
Practice being at peace in the chaos.

Being at peace is the ultimate expression of Quiet Mind Epic Life. It takes practice.

To achieve it, you will learn to catch The Drunk Monkey reacting and choose your response instead. If The Drunk Monkey is in reaction, then there is no peace.

Practice being at peace in the middle of chaos today. You can be at peace if you choose it. It will take practice, but it is achievable.

You feel overwhelmed by chaos when you are unconscious and The Drunk Monkey is trying to protect you. It robs you of clarity and perspective and dominates your mental state.

It's only chaos because of your resistance to it. Chaos is a label you give to something that puts you out of balance. Today let go of your resistance to feeling out of control. In fact, embrace the feeling of being out of control.

Like a surfer on the wave, give into the power that is greater than you and ride the energy of it. The only reason things feel fast or out of control is because you are resisting it. Smile. Shake your head yes. Laugh at the insanity of life, people and situations.

What first appears as ugly and chaotic, can suddenly appear to be beauty, art, and perfection. You get to choose.

If things are breaking down. If there are disasters happening in your life. If you are losing what you want. If you are being limited by life. Embrace it. Make the best of it. Enjoy the limitation. Ride the wave of the breakdown like the surfer.

When the surfer wipes out on a wave, they go limp. They give themselves over to the wave completely. They let the wave take them until the energy dissipates and they can escape easily. If the surfer resists, they waste energy and it uses oxygen. They know they cannot beat the sea. This is the same for you.

You are not in charge of the situation. Yes, you can influence it. You can sometimes direct it. But most of the time even that is an illusion. Most of the time you are the one experiencing what is happening, pretending like you are the controller of it.

When things are chaotic, get excited. Change is afoot. Something good is happening. Breakdown is the beginning of breakthrough.

Napoleon Hill said it like this, "There is a seed of equivalent benefit in every adversity." But that seed lies dormant until you create the conditions for the breakthrough to occur. Those conditions are ingenuity, creativity, and resourcefulness. Those conditions happen when you are in a flow state and they are repressed when you resist.

Be in a state of peace and calm even when life doesn't meet your expectations. Remember that your expectations of life, people and circumstances are just made up stories. They aren't real. The Drunk Monkey is pretending that it is psychic and knows how life should be. The Drunk Monkey is pretending to be the ruler of the universe and force people to live by its doctrine.

You don't know anything. You are doing the best you can to make sense of a world that doesn't make sense. Logic is a figment of our imagination. A likely story. Plausible at best. Life consistently breaks with logic and then we invent some new story to explain that.

Life is doing what it is doing. Embrace it.

As you embrace Enlightened Perspectives, you get to choose your experience of life. You are no longer at the effect of life. That is real freedom. That is what creates Quiet Mind Epic Life.

Day 13 Enlightened Perspectives

- Chaos is just a label I give to a set of conditions I'm experiencing.
- I am not the ruler of the universe. I am the observer of the energy and information my senses are picking up.
- I am the interpreter and my interpretations are creating the reality I am experiencing.

Day 14 Practice
Recognize the prosperity that is all around you.

You are on your way to enjoying Quiet Mind Epic Life. It takes practice. It takes intention. It takes awareness.

When you recognize the prosperity that is all around you, you feel more at ease. That's because you are pointing your awareness in a direction that demonstrates to The Drunk Monkey that all is well.

When you show The Drunk Monkey the incredible abundance that surrounds you, it's less apt to engage Greed and fear that there won't be enough to go around.

Today push yourself to recognize the prosperity that is already in your life right now. You are living in the most abundant time in human history. You are living in such radical abundance that you are focused on Self-Actualization at the top of Maslow's Hierarchy of Needs.

Get this into perspective: Your physiological needs are handled. You aren't focused on whether or not if you will have enough food, water, shelter or rest today.

You aren't focused on your safety and security. You already feel a sense of belonging. You are transcending your need to feel like you are important or successful.

You are literally working on self-actualization; the achievement of one's full potential through creativity, independence, and personal responsibility.

Holy smokes! You are standing at the top of the pyramid having the profound realization that all you really want is to feel joy, certainty, love, and fulfillment. You recognize that happiness is the whole enchilada. What a luxury.

To make things even more powerful, you have realized that money doesn't make you happy. Success doesn't make you happy. Things don't make you happy. Not even happy people make you happy.

You thought money, success, marriage, children, holidays, cars, and stuff would make you happy. But now you know that the real prize was simply happiness.

You are one of the luckiest and most prosperous people on the planet because you have realized that an effective context is the only thing that will make you happy. Nothing out there in the world will do the trick.

This makes you a person who has an incredible abundance, advantage, prosperity, and access to the most sought-after resource in the world... Happiness.

Just drink it in today. Get giddy about how lucky you are.

As you embrace Enlightened Perspectives, you get to choose your experience of life. You are no longer at the effect of life. That is real freedom. That is what creates Quiet Mind Epic Life.

Day 14 Enlightened Perspectives

- The world is perfect exactly as it is. All is well.

- I am living in greater states of abundance than ever before in human history. All is well.

- Even if nothing changes. All is well.

- Even if I never achieve or create anything. All is well.

Day 15 Practice
Accept what you have, focus on what you want; be satisfied and eager for more.

Your mind talks because it is trying to solve problems that don't exist. It is holding you accountable to arbitrary benchmarks that aren't being achieved. This causes dissatisfaction; which activates even more mind chatter. This is an endless cycle of never feeling satisfied. To counter this phenomenon, accept what you have and be eager for more.

Your energy and enthusiasm will explode into joy and delight when you take the time to fully accept that what you have now is perfect.

When you are filled with exuberance, your creativity, resourcefulness and focused energy will rise up and you will start taking action on your new desires.

When you are satisfied and eager for more, your mind goes quiet and your life gets epic.

Where you are, right now, is the perfect jumping off point for what is next in your life. Really get connected to the feeling that all is well in the world. In fact, just because you want to change your life right now, doesn't make it wrong.

The only thing that makes now wrong is your label. Why would you label it in a way that makes you feel bad, shuts down your creativity and causes you to feel limited?

If you are going to make things up, why not make things up that feel good?

Be satisfied with how life is right now and then be eager for more.

Notice how you actually have everything you need right now. You are literally a conversation or two away from opening doors, getting resources, and the help that you need to manifest just about anything you can dream up.

You already know this because of what you already have. You currently have everything you have been focusing on in the past in some form. Your focus turns into real results and real tangible changes. It might take longer than you want. But that's just The Drunk Monkey making up some arbitrary rule about time frames. You are not the ruler of the universe. You don't know how it is all supposed to go. You don't know what is right or wrong. You just know what you want.

If you make now wrong, you create the opposite energy necessary to create what you want.

Today just be satisfied and eager for more.

As you embrace Enlightened Perspectives, you get to choose your experience of life. You are no longer at the effect of life. That is real freedom. That is what creates Quiet Mind Epic Life.

Day 15 Enlightened Perspectives

- My life is perfect exactly as it is.

- All is well.

- Nothing needs to change for me to accept that I'm in a state of perfection right now.

Day 16 Practice
Marvel at the perfection of life.

When you learn to marvel at the perfection of life, you disengage the need for The Drunk Monkey, your mind goes quiet and you set yourself up for an epic life.

You get to choose your experience of life. Nothing needs to change for you to be delighted. And why would you choose anything other than awe, delight, and joy anyway?

As a matter of principle, I want you to marvel at the perfection of life today. It ain't nothin' 'til you call it. So call it something that is uplifting and inspiring.

If you step back and get really honest with yourself today, you can admit that you don't actually know why life is the way it is. You don't know how it got this way. You don't know what the source of the plants, animals, land masses, water, or humans are.

Sure we can make up a story about it. But that's all we have. Why not admit it. You are full of lies and assumptions about everything. You don't know why anything is the way it is. And with that huge relief, you can just be in awe of the way it all is.

Life is exactly the way it is. It's not good, bad, right or wrong. That's all you and your value judgments. Step back and notice the perfection of it all. Notice the marvelous way everything works together. Notice the harmony in the chaos. Notice the peace in the noise. The inter-connectivity. The beauty, the horrific, the lovely, and the nasty. Notice the amazing variety of expressions on the planet. Just be present.

Then notice the perfection of your life experiences. Notice the perfection of your lot in life. Notice the perfection of your circumstances.

Then just reflect on this idea. You are in pursuit of a quiet mind and an epic life. That is a pursuit that implies all your other needs are met. Reflect on how perfect your life is right now.

Consider that the good, bad and ugly are all leading you on a journey of ever-increasing abundance and prosperity. Because the prosperity you seek is one of well-being.

Your opinion about life determines your experience of it. Create opinions that cause you to marvel at the perfection of it all.

As you embrace Enlightened Perspectives, you get to choose your experience of life. You are no longer at the effect of life. That is real freedom. That is what creates Quiet Mind Epic Life.

Day 16 Enlightened Perspectives

- Incarnating on Earth is like my soul taking a vacation from being infinite.

- Life is whole, complete and perfect exactly as it is.

Day 17 Practice
Embrace and celebrate breakdown.

Quiet Mind Epic Life is not possible when you are resisting the way that your life is. When things go wrong, objectives don't get achieved or, when you want life to be something other than it is, I call that a breakdown.

Today I want you to consider this Recontextualization: Take stock of past breakdowns. Notice how they all, eventually, lead to a better and better experience of life.

Every breakdown you have ever had in your life has turned into a breakthrough somewhere else in your life. Destruction and creation are the same things just at different stages of the process.

When something is failing. When an idea isn't working. When your relationship is falling apart. Embrace and celebrate the breakdown.

Breakdown leads to breakthrough. Breakdowns only feel bad because The Drunk Monkey gets attached to losing an exaggerated benefit or experiencing an exaggerated negative.

Bust The Drunk Monkey. It doesn't know the future. You are not psychic. Your survival mind has evolved into a prediction machine. But it is far from accurate. And the predictions never take into account your creativity and ingenuity. But you can't even access those parts of your consciousness if you are in fight or flight.

Just say this to yourself over and over today, "Breakdown is the beginning of breakthrough." Breakdown is the other side of the coin of breakthrough.

In fact, if you look closely at a person who is having success, you will see that it's the result of handling breakdowns effectively over and over and over.

When my father asked his mentor, Earl Nightingale what success was like, his answer was telling. He told my father, "Success is like standing in a hammock on one leg, juggling 12 eggs."

Think about that for a second. How many times will you fall just trying to stand on one leg in a hammock? Hundreds? Thousands? Each fall, stumble, and fail is leading to the ultimate success of being able to stand on one leg in a hammock.

Success is a series of well-managed breakdowns. The breakdown is the journey. What feels like breakdown in the moment is seen as necessary in hindsight.

Whatever your objective might be, failure, breakdown, and obstacles will be the process to fulfill it. If you want to be promoted at work and you get passed over. That's part of the process of getting promoted. If you are committed to having a quiet mind and The Drunk Monkey won't shut up, that's part of your process to achieving quiet mind.

There are no bad goals, just bad deadlines. It's all happening in perfect time. It takes as long as it takes. You are not the ruler of the Universe! The Drunk Monkey enforces arbitrary deadlines that don't exist. Then when you don't accomplish your objective in the made-up timeline, you feel like a failure. It's only a breakdown because of the arbitrary rule The Drunk Monkey created. It's not a breakdown in reality.

You just need to make peace with the fact that it's always going your way even when it's not. Will you just get over your victim BS and recognize that you are living a blessed life?

Today practice appreciating all that is going wrong in your life. Trust that the changes you want are coming. All there is to do is focus on the perfection of right now, regain your clarity and move forward.

As you embrace Enlightened Perspectives, you get to choose your experience of life. You are no longer at the effect of life. That is real freedom. That is what creates Quiet Mind Epic Life.

Day 17 Enlightened Perspectives

- Failure is just a perspective.
- Failure is just a broken expectation.
- Failure isn't final unless I declare it so.
- Destruction and creation are the same things just at different stages.

Day 18 Practice
Set your intention and detach from the outcome.

Your mind will go quiet and that will lead to an epic life when you practice detachment.

The Drunk Monkey gets attached. It fears that arbitrary, made up results won't happen in the future. When it is planning, strategizing and freaking out about the loss of future results, your mind is not quiet.

Let's Recontextualize today. Try this on. If you want it, then it's coming. You can't want it unless it is already a probability that you are tuned to. You don't need to fret about it.

I'm predisposed to music so new musical ideas come into my consciousness all the time. I write them down. Some turn into something. Most don't.

I'm predisposed to spiritual investigation and developing myself. New ideas on how to do that pop into my consciousness all the time. Some I work on. Others I don't.

Whatever you intend on happening is not your idea. You don't own it. It's a probability field of consciousness that you are a part of. You are a part of the Universe's propensity to manifest. You are a tool for the Universe to bring things into this world.

For example, you have set your intention to have Quiet Mind Epic Life. Not everyone cares about that. Not everyone is predisposed to that kind of intention. You are. And the very fact that you are this far into the book is evidence that you are a good fit for this intention.

It's coming. Your job is to create the conditions conducive to its full manifestation in your life. Don't get attached to the process. It will happen for you in a completely different way than it happened for me. It will happen for you in a completely different way than it happened for all my students before you.

Practice detaching from how you think things should be. Let go of the idea that you know how it's supposed to happen when it's supposed to happen and what's going to happen. It's all conjecture. It's all made up.

When things don't go your way, and they won't, The Drunk Monkey will engage. Practice noticing this happening.

When you get disturbed by The Drunk Monkey, don't get alarmed. Don't resist it. Don't fight it. Don't try to squash it. Just know that you are on the right path.

Don't pretend you have all the answers. You don't. Don't pretend that this book is "the answer" because it's not. It's just my best foot forward at describing what has been a nearly indescribable process for me and my clients.

Let go of your ideas about how it's all supposed to go and surrender to the flow. Enjoy the process. Enjoy the ups and the downs. Be the surfer on the ocean. Some days the waves are big and some days there are no waves and everything in between. Don't pretend you can control the world.

Set your intention for enlightened consciousness to flow through you. Just keep doing that over and over every day. Then notice, be present and be curious. It's coming. You never know how it will show up.

As you embrace Enlightened Perspectives, you get to choose your experience of life. You are no longer at the effect of life. That is real freedom. That is what creates Quiet Mind Epic Life.

Day 18 Enlightened Perspectives

- I am the background quantum field of energy and information manifesting into reality.
- All of my ideas, goals, projects, and intentions are an expression of the source.
- My ideas are manifesting through me.
- I am the manifestation.

Day 19 Practice
Remember that there are no rules in life.

To achieve Quiet Mind Epic Life, remember that there are no rules in life. Every rule you follow is made up. Which doesn't mean that "actual rules" don't exist. They do. If you break the rule of walking into a busy street when the crosswalk signal indicates that it's not safe to cross, then you risk get hit by a car. Those aren't the kinds of rules I'm talking about.

The Drunk Monkey makes up rules that limit you. You can recognize them because they contain: should, shouldn't, have to, must, need to.

The Drunk Monkey's rules are arbitrary conditioning that doesn't exist in the real world. But you follow them like they are real. "I have to get married and have kids." That's a made-up rule that many people follow.

"If you don't respond to my text message right away then something is wrong." Not true but a disturbing rule that many people have.

Do this today. Notice the places in your life where you feel limited. Then use your awareness to pierce through the illusions and figure out which Illogical Rules are holding you back.

Noticing is step one in releasing them. Awareness makes you flexible; which reveals new options and gives you power.

Just identifying the Illogical Rules you are following will create the conditions to quickly move past them and become empowered.

In general, question everything. Don't just blindly do what you are told. Don't just fall into line because that's what you were told to do. Don't just toe the family line because that's what everyone expects you to do. The odds of achieving a quiet mind are dramatically diminished by that.

Today just test what happens when you stop following the social protocols that don't make you feel good. Don't tell anyone. Just do it. Be a scientist and notice the result. Stop being a sheep. Instead, seek to rise above cultural conditioning, limiting dogma and unexamined beliefs.

Today, release anything you are doing out of guilt or obligation. Guilt is a feeling that has been trained into you. It's a negative cocktail of fears and resentments. You fear losing a benefit. You resent having to comply. It's all based on an illusion.

Don't be so arrogant to believe that YOU are going to hurt your mom's feelings if you don't come to dinner. You can't hurt her feelings. Only she has the power to hurt herself. If you are going to have a quiet mind, then you are going to have to recognize that everyone is on their own journey and there is nothing you can do about it. You are not in charge of anyone else's happiness.

When you stop following protocols that don't make you feel good, people will try to talk you back into being compliant. Practice honoring their perspective. Have deep respect and reverence for the value of their protocols. And gracefully and respectfully decline without resisting, without justifying, without rationalizing.

Today release any measurement or arbitrary rule about how life should be based on the past. Just because it happened in the past, doesn't mean it will happen again in the future. There are infinite probabilities playing out. Set your intention to have Quiet Mind Epic Life and then let go of all your rules and measurements.

As you embrace Enlightened Perspectives, you get to choose your experience of life. You are no longer at the effect of life. That is real freedom. That is what creates Quiet Mind Epic Life.

Day 19 Enlightened Perspectives

- The rules don't apply to me.

- I don't need to moderate my actions in an effort to make sure I am taking positive and constructive actions.

- I am the part of the human species that defaults to taking positive and constructive actions.

- All I have to do is release the illusion that I'm going to survive and I will naturally take positive uplifting action.

Day 20 Practice
Notice that your mind is not your friend.

Quiet Mind Epic Life is an expression of your intention to be enlightened. Being enlightened is simply a heightened state of awareness. It's a non-resistant state where you allow all things to be exactly as they are. It's a perspective that creates the conditions for profound happiness and peace no matter what life is doing.

Today, set the intention for enlightened consciousness to flow through you. Set the intention to recognize that your mind, The Drunk Monkey, is not your friend.

The Drunk Monkey doesn't care about you and what you want. It doesn't care about enlightenment. It doesn't care about having a quiet mind or an epic life.

The Drunk Monkey doesn't even like you. Just notice that today. Notice that it doesn't have nice things to say about you. You look in the mirror and it has an opinion about this or that and it's not very uplifting.

The Drunk Monkey doesn't care about you or your objectives. It will talk you out of doing what you want for fear of being uncomfortable, embarrassed or losing something it's already comfortable with. It's the mouthpiece of the survival mind and you keep listening to it like it's on your side.

Stop listening to The Drunk Monkey like a trusted advisor. It's not. There's no doubt that it is a strategist. It's a problem solver. But it will spend countless hours obsessing over problems that don't even exist. It will invent future conversations with people you might not even encounter. It will waste your time repeating back the latest economic news.

Today get connected to its motives. It believes you are at a disadvantage. It wants to avoid being put in a bad position. It wants to look good, be right, and be valued.

If it can't get people to value it through being good, then it will intentionally be a victim to try and get people to take care of you through pity.

Your mind is not your friend. It doesn't care about your intention to be enlightened. It doesn't care about your goal to have an epic life. Asking your mind to participate in those activities is like expecting a car engine to brew coffee. Wrong machine to produce the desired outcome.

As you embrace Enlightened Perspectives, you get to choose your experience of life. You are no longer at the effect of life. That is real freedom. That is what creates a Quiet Mind Epic Life.

Day 20 Enlightened Perspectives

- Unwanted mental chatter is a biological system.
- I am not the talking in my head.

- I am aware of the talking.
- The talking doesn't represent reality, only possibilities.

Day 21 Practice
Remove language that justifies degrading realities.

To achieve your objective of living with a quiet mind and having an epic life, you must become a master of language.

The Drunk Monkey is reacting to the language you use to relate to life. The Drunk Monkey has its own set of habitual language patterns that turn you into a victim of life.

The reality you are living is very simply the language you are using to describe the situation.

Today practice removing the language that justifies a degrading experience and start using language that empowers you.

To shift the power from The Drunk Monkey back to you requires you to deconstruct the language you use to describe everything.

There is no such thing as explaining or describing. You are always creating. When you are explaining something, don't make the mistake of thinking you are explaining "the" reality of the situation. You are not. You are explaining your perspective.

Your reality seems more and more real to you because of the language you use, the repetitious thoughts that program your reality and the people who parrot back the descriptions you use.

In fact, consider this idea. If people didn't explain and describe things the way you did, you would have troubles with them. They would feel offensive, repelling or annoying. Why? Because their version of reality contradicted your reality; which activates The Drunk Monkey.

Notice that you aren't explaining anything. You are giving your opinion. You aren't describing anything. You are giving your opinion. Can you imagine if we had ten people describe this book? There would be ten different descriptions with only a few similarities. The language used would be extremely diverse.

Today, begin to change your perspective about explaining and describing things. Imagine that you are actually creating a reality. One for yourself and one for the people you are talking to.

Practice choosing the reality you want and describing things in a way that creates your ideal reality. I'm not asking you to be impractical or inaccurate. I'm asking you to choose your words with the intention of being empowered.

Your descriptions of what happened aren't the reality of what happened. They are your opinions. They are a story you made up about the situation. If you are going to make things up, why not make things up that feel good?

Here are some questions you can ask yourself today:

1. Why do I call it that?

2. Why am I describing it this way?

3. Am I getting a negative payoff?

4. Am I making myself out to be the victim?

5. Am I intentionally hiding things?

6. What else can I say about it?

7. Is this perspective serving me?

8. What can say that will empower me?

As you embrace Enlightened Perspectives, you get to choose your experience of life. You are no longer at the effect of life. That is real freedom. That is what creates Quiet Mind Epic Life.

Day 21 Enlightened Perspectives

- God doesn't care or have an opinion on anything.

- I am whole, complete and perfect exactly as I am.

- The only things that are wrong with me are arbitrary illogical perceptions.

- All is well.

- We are all the same thing expressing itself with infinite variety.

Day 22 Practice
Your opinion is the source of your suffering.

A quiet mind is a mind that has no opinions. When you see your opinion for what it is, you are able to step back from limiting beliefs and take steps towards creating an epic life. That takes practice.

The Drunk Monkey has an opinion on everything including things it knows nothing about.

Don't get down on The Drunk Monkey. It's not a bad thing. It's a good thing. The Drunk Monkey is like the Central Intelligence Agency (The CIA) of The United States. Its job is to seek out potential threats and then avoid them. That biological process has been a blessing to the whole of humanity.

You are here in this place because The Drunk Monkey assesses, analyzes, and formulates opinions on everything it is exposed to.

Your ancestors' Drunk Monkeys created tool after tool making the world safe, abundant and comfortable. That all came about by forming opinions and then executing on hypothetical futures.

But now you have a problem. Your needs are met. You have climbed to the top of the proverbial mountain only to discover that life is whole, complete and perfect exactly as it is. You have relative safety, food, shelter, self-expression, and esteem. That is all thanks to The Drunk Monkey.

But now you are working to transcend the very thing that got you here. To achieve Quiet Mind Epic Life you must relinquish the obligation to comment on everything. You must release your duties as the chief describer of everything.

In the end, your opinions are just vanities with no value to anyone. They are your perspective. They are your opinion. They aren't better or worse than anyone else's.

Giving your opinion and being attached to your perspective stems from ignorance. Only an insecure person needs to be right about their perspective. Being attached to your opinion is a guaranteed way to create conflict, fights, arguments, and disagreements.

If you don't feel good, it's because of your opinion. You are resisting the way that things are. The discourse of that resistance is called suffering. The pressure you feel in your body that you call a negative emotion is being generated in response to a mismatch of your opinion compared to what's actually happening.

When you feel negative emotions, that's a signal to release your opinion. That's a signal that you are focusing on something that isn't working for you. Suffering is a signal that you are resisting.

Opinions are the source of suffering. Practice releasing your opinions today. Be in the flow. Honor the many perspectives of the people around you.

That doesn't mean you are going to be irresponsible. If you are the leader in a situation and your opinion is what matters to the people around you, then give it. Just release any resistance to other opinions. Don't be attached. Be open to the myriad of possibilities that are available in any given moment.

As you embrace Enlightened Perspectives, you get to choose your experience of life. You are no longer at the effect of life. That is real freedom. That is what creates Quiet Mind Epic Life.

Day 22 Enlightened Perspectives

- Opinions are the source of my suffering.

- Opinions are arbitrary.

- I do not know what reality is.

- All I have is the interpretation of the energy and information that I am perceiving using my five senses.

- If I'm going to make things up, I might as well make up stories that are empowering and feel good.

Day 23 Practice
You are not psychic. You don't know what the future holds.

To create a Quiet Mind Epic Life you have to admit that you don't know what the future holds. You must embrace the unknown and stay committed to being open and flexible.

Today practice that you are not psychic. Keep admitting that you don't know what the future holds.

You must learn to catch The Drunk Monkey creating negative futures that it intends to avoid. The stress of an imaginary negative future will disturb your quiet mind and it takes your focus off creating your epic life.

The Drunk Monkey is unconcerned with your quiet mind and doesn't care about creating an epic life.

The Drunk Monkey is just doing its job. It's trying to estimate what will happen to move you into the best possible position. It's a biological survival system. Its programmed to avoid negative outcomes and seek positive ones. That's great news for all of us. Until you want to create a quiet mind with an epic life.

Today challenge The Drunk Monkey. Start to ask the question, "How do you know that will happen?" Put The Drunk Monkey to the test by creating experiments.

Rather than fearing a negative future or pretending you know what will happen, find out. Discover the truth rather than pretending to know the truth. The only responsible thing to do is to move forward and find out what will happen.

Be detached rather than fearful. Be curious rather than assumptive. Be open rather than pretending you already know the outcome. This will begin to quiet the mind.

When The Drunk Monkey is lamenting an imaginary negative future, force its hand. Challenge The Drunk Monkey to do a contingency plan. Take control and imagine the worst possible thing can happen. The Drunk Monkey will hate this and resist. It is afraid of what might happen. Grab it by the ear and drag it through the process of looking at the absolute worst thing that could happen.

Once you have created your vision of the worst possible outcome, then create a plan to move forward from that place. Don't let The Drunk Monkey try to distract you with plans to avoid the worst. Force it to accept the worst case scenario action plan.

The mind will almost immediately go quiet. The pressure of that imaginary future will be gone. Then be ready for the rush of creativity and resourcefulness. That's when it comes. When you acknowledge that you are capable of handling the bad stuff, your courage, creativity, and resourcefulness naturally rise.

Getting upset about imaginary negative futures is just stupid. The Drunk Monkey is not psychic. You don't know what the future holds.

As you learn to shut down The Drunk Monkey and take conscious control of your response, you will more effortlessly control your future. Which doesn't mean you will always avoid negative outcomes. But as you reach higher levels of consciousness, the miraculous not only become commonplace, it can be continuous.

The future is just a made up story. Why not makeup stories that feel good?

As you embrace Enlightened Perspectives, you get to choose your experience of life. You are no longer at the effect of life. That is real freedom. That is what creates Quiet Mind Epic Life.

Day 23 Enlightened Perspectives

- I am not psychic. I don't know the future.
- All I have is this moment.
- All estimations of the future are just foolish fantasies.
- All is well.
- I am capable of handling anything that comes my way.

Day 23 Practice: You are not psychic. You don't know what the future holds.

Congratulations
You have the tools to create your own unique Quiet Mind Epic Life

The Rapid Enlightenment Process is a series of contextual shifts that destroy cultural conditioning, limiting dogma and unexamined beliefs and replaces them with new enlightened dogma aka Enlightened Perspectives.

At the beginning of Quiet Mind Epic Life, I made a very audacious claim. I stated that *"The ability to master the process that I will teach you in this book will free you from ever having to read another self-help book. Ever. Unless you are inspired to do so."*

I stand by that claim.

The pages of Quiet Mind Epic Life contain the proven process I've used to free myself and my clients from the survival mind and ascend into an enlightened state.

When you seek to understand the nature of The Drunk Monkey and it Unconsciousness Reflexes, you see that you are not your thoughts. Most likely when you started this book, that was a familiar paradigm.

Going further, I revealed to you SOURCE of The Drunk Monkey's opinions, concerns, judgments, and doomsday predictions: The Hidden Motives To Survive.

On your journey to Quiet Mind Epic Life, it's vital that you understand, and ultimately eliminate, the impact of the Hidden Motives in your life. When the Hidden Motives are released, the motive for thinking is removed. The Drunk Monkey loses its job, and intuition and inspiration become your guides.

Enlightened Perspectives are the key. When you are able to create an empowering context, regardless of the circumstances you find yourself in, you are free. Recontextualization is a master skill. I've given you a series of Enlightened Perspectives throughout this book along with 23 Daily Practices to ensure you have a way to consistently return to an all is well state.

Thank you for joining me on the Quiet Mind Epic Life journey.

I look forward to our paths crossing again.

- Matthew

Congratulations: You have the tools to create your own unique Quiet Mind Epic Life

Appendix A
The Worst Case Scenario

A quiet mind is an expression of being worry-free. It's knowing that all is well; which is the foundation of the enlightened state. Your mind goes quiet when you know that you are not in a survival state. This is not easy to achieve because The Drunk Monkey has an Unconscious Reflex called Forecasting The Negative.

In spite of what The Drunk Monkey says, you don't know what the future will hold. But that doesn't stop The Drunk Monkey from making up stories and repeating them to you over and over. You can't count on The Drunk Monkey to present you with positive and optimistic futures. That's not its job. It is a survival mechanism.

The most effective thing you can do to combat The Drunk Monkey is to face it, confront it, and remove its motivation for being activated in the first place. The Worst Case Scenario Exercise does just that. You are going to face your worst fears and make plans to move forward once they happen. If you try to avoid them, they clutter up your mind with negative futures.

Here are the steps.

1. Write out the worst case scenario you are avoiding. Intentionally make it bad. The Drunk Monkey is ruthless and doesn't care about being rational. So indulge the sur-

vival mind. Go to the extremes. If you can think of it, then you have thought of it in the past and The Drunk Monkey is afraid of it. I'm not kidding. Make your story about the worst case scenario absurd.

2. Read this worst case scenario out loud to yourself over and over again.

3. Keep reading it until you start to see that it is just a made up story.

4. This is the most important step. Make peace with this absurd story happening. The way you do this is by making a plan to move forward after the worst case scenario happens.

Do not allow The Drunk Monkey to derail you on this process. It will try to distract you with plans to avoid the worst case. Don't let it do that. Face the worst case scenario head-on. Look at it in detail. Then make your plan to move forward once that terrible future happens.

This process is not fun or enjoyable. You will not like the idea of allowing the worst case scenario to happen. This will not feel good. I'm asking you to plan for the worst case scenario so that you can make peace with it as one possible outcome.

What you resist will persist. What you accept will transform.

When you resist the worst case scenario, you keep it fixed in place. It keeps flashing in your mind and influencing your actions based on avoiding and fear. When you accept it and plan for it, there is no more need to think about it. You have your plan. This gives rise to insights and ideas that were not available in your retracted fearful state.

When you make peace with The Worst Case Scenario, you can experience "all is well." This is vital to maintaining your quiet mind.

Appendix B
Release Attachment Exercise

Attachment is an exaggerated fear of losing an imaginary benefit. Attachment is the fear of losing something before you even have it.

In a nutshell, when you are afraid to take action, you are likely attached to losing an imaginary benefit.

When you are attached, you are afraid. When you are afraid you are inflexible. When you are attached and things don't go as expected you might panic or feel frustrated. Panic and frustration limit your flexibility, reduces your options and kills your personal power. These are expressions of the survival mind.

You know you are attached when you say things like...

I can't do that!

What will people think?

I'm not that kind of person.

I never get it right.

Other people can do that, but not me.

Each of those statements implies limitation and the fear that something valuable might be lost if you take action.

This is distinct from being committed. When you are committed, you are open to whatever happens and eager to keep moving forward regardless of the obstacles you might encounter. When you are committed, you know that all is well. This creates openness and peace of mind.

When you connect with Enlightened Perspectives you don't judge. You don't make things wrong. You operate like a scientist. You are curious and interested. The scientist admits that they don't know what will happen. The scientist is committed to exploring every idea possible to create the desired result. Each failure just creates clarity and deeper understanding. Failure is just learning. It's part of the process.

When you are committed, you are unattached to how it all happens. You are dedicated but you aren't fearful. You have the personal power to see it through regardless of the path. Unattached to the outcome. Which doesn't mean you are passive. You accept the situation as it is and then move from there. You don't get stopped by your results.

Attachment is the opposite of flexibility. Attachment creates a fixed reality where the outcome is known and not changeable. This perspective is an illusion. It is the result of seeing the world through the survival mind.

Flexibility is your greatest asset. You don't know what's going to happen. You don't know the path you are going to take. You have ideas but those ideas are just possibilities, not the truth. You don't know the perfect process.

Commit to releasing your attachment, right now. Release The Drunk Monkey's arrogant perspective that the future is known. Stay open to whatever happens. Laugh, enjoy the process and declare the results, positive or negative, perfect.

If you are attached, you get upset when things don't go as expected and you become inflexible. Attachment limits your options, creativity, and power.

To free yourself from the limitation of attachment, use my Release Attachment Exercise.

- Step 1: Write out what action you are afraid to take. Where are feeling stuck?

- Step 2: Write down what benefit you are afraid of losing if you take action.

- Step 3: Be extremely honest with yourself. If you have written down step one and two this will be much easier. If you are doing this in your head, it will be more challenging. Write down all the reasons why your fear is exaggerated.

- Step 4: Write out how losing the benefit would actually affect you without the exaggeration. Get brass tacks. Be really clear and concise. Take all the fearful language out of your description.

- Step 5: Write down what you will do if you don't get the benefit. In the process make peace with the loss of the benefit.

- Step 6: Write down a new intention for yourself now that you have released your attachment.

- Step 7: Write down your promises to yourself. How will you know that you are being committed and flexible vs. attached and stuck? Write out the attitudes, perspectives, context, and actions you will take to demonstrate your commitment.

Releasing attachment is a powerful way to get The Drunk Monkey to shut up. It aligns you with the Enlightened Perspective that all is well. I encourage you to follow this process everytime you feel stuck.

About The Author
Matthew Ferry

Matthew Ferry's promise is simple: Quiet your mind so you can create an epic life, that is filled with Enlightened Prosperity. His down to earth approach empowers you to rise above the unwanted chatter and negativity of the mind. Matthew says, "When your mind is quiet, you feel profound peace and your life becomes extraordinary. No ashram required."

For the last 25 years, Matthew has been coaching thousands of top performers to achieve Enlightened Prosperity. His books, audios and seminars utilize his street tested methodology called The Rapid Enlightenment Process; a guaranteed system to achieve a quiet mind.

Feedback and comments about Quiet Mind Epic Life welcomed. Please send an email to mferry@matthewferry.com

Learn more about Matthew, his programs and live events online at:

matthewferry.com

blog.matthewferry.com

Special Message
From The Author

My Journey to Enlightenment was longer than yours needs to be.

I remember when it happened the first time. I was nine years old and suddenly, I was floating 100 feet above the book that I was reading. I wasn't actually floating. I could still feel my body but my experience was like nothing I'd ever felt before.

Bliss, joy, perfection, courage jolted through my body like a sunset that takes your breath away. I was overcome with the feeling of perfection. I hoped it would never end. But then, as quickly as it happened, it was gone.

Dread took over. I didn't want to feel the confusion of being a nine year old. The discomfort and the insecurities of being a human being were thrown in my face by the contrast. I wanted the bliss and the courage back.

As I grew, the feeling never left me. For that brief moment I knew that all was well. There was nothing to fear. All the rules were bullshit. The protocols, the cultural norms, right, wrong, good and bad. It was all a lie. In that place I was whole, complete and perfect exactly as I was. Nothing needed to change.

Starting in my teens, I did everything I could to find that feeling again. Sex, drugs, being popular, success, houses, cars, and money. None of it worked.

I didn't know it at the time but I was looking for enlightenment in all the wrong places.

The Rapid Enlightenment Process is the result of my journey to find the bliss, joy, perfection, and courage as felt when I was 9.

As you engage The Rapid Enlightenment Process, you experience a series of contextual shifts that destroy cultural conditioning, limiting dogma and unexamined beliefs, and replaces them with new enlightened dogma aka Enlightened Perspectives.

When experiencing Enlightened Perspectives your essence is shining. You are doing well personally, professionally, relationally, mentally, spiritually, and financially. Everything is working. You are unlimited. You are free.

This is what I want for you.

Thank you for joining me on this journey.

Ways To Engage
Join our Community!

Experience The Rapid Enlightenment Process first hand at Matthew Ferry's Epic Life Live. Find event dates and locations at epiclifelive.com

Join Matthew's Spiritual Hooligan Closed Facebook Group at facebook.com/groups/spiritualhooligans

Made in the USA
Middletown, DE
18 August 2019